LYNEE PALACIOS'

INSPIRE

A CURATED GUIDE ON LOVE, LIFE, AND
EVERYTHING IN BETWEEN

*'When you know who you are, there'll be no doubt on where
you're going*

—LYNEE PALACIOS

ISBN: 978-0-578-94424-1

Imprint: Independently Published

Cover layout by: Amber Castañeda & MyVIAA, LLC

Edited by: Kathryn Tague

To my Mom, Anna,
whose love and grace never once wavered,
& to Charlee.
My little one, one day you'll read this with a smile
and know you've been loved
even before you were born.

Contents

Acknowledgments

My deepest gratitude to:

Those who believed in me and never gave up on my
dreams nor doubted my abilities.

To my loving and ever-supportive siblings, Lisa,
Valerie, Francisco, and Fabian. To my parents, Frank
and Anna, for raising the 5 of us and keeping us
together. To my life and business mentors, Tony
Robbins, Dean Graziosi, Aaron Garrity, and Jamie Kern
Lima. To my loving life partner, Jerome Drake. To my
loving stepson, William. To all the No's I got and the
doors that have closed, to all the hardships that have
made me who I am today, to all the wins in my life. To
my MB30 days, living a limitless lifestyle. To the KBB
Family, my Wonder Women Mastery tribe, my VIAA
Family, and my Intuitive Moms.

And my deepest gratitude to my Higher Self, the
Universe, and God.

This book was born out of love. I hope you enjoy it as
much as I've enjoyed sharing my heart with you and

inspiring you to act and become the best version of
yourself.

Foreword

As an author, educator, and innovator in the self-education industry, I've spent my life collecting and sharing stories that inspire myself and others to action. Action to grow, evolve and become who we are meant to be. We all can grow through these valuable narratives and that these stories are the fabric that links us all together in this journey called life. Throughout my life journey, I've been blessed to be surrounded by people whose stories fueled me and my company with the strength and new beliefs.

For decades, I've worked with individuals whose commitment to service contributed to the overall narrative of the company. One of them is Lynee, who served as our community manager and director. She became one of our front liners in the field, managing the company's online community and committing herself to its growth. Along the way, I've been a witness to her amazing journey as a person. Her vibrant passion for life and commitment to service, along with her unrelenting and contagious positivity, provided us with grit and motivation. She pours her passion and soul into everything she does, as she did writing this book, *Inspire.*

Just as she offers inspiration and encouragement in life, every page of her book is filled with insight drawn from her colorful story. What amazed me most about this book is how Lynee was able to weave together the culmination of her life journey-both triumphs and defeats, hoping to inspire others to go out there and do the same. *Inspire*, is a book committed to leading its readers to take action, take the helm of their fate, and change their lives. Just as Lynee's passion and enthusiasm amazed me, I hope that you'll get inspired and excited as you read her book full of wisdom and motivation. Read this book and prepare to drink from the stream of inspiration, guidance, and tools that will help you discover ways to take control of your life.

As Lynee would say, "You hold the key to your success. You are the author of your destiny." So, start your personal journey towards a balanced life. *Inspire*, becomes your entryway to the life you deserve.

Dean Graziosi, Multiple New York Times Best-Selling Author of, *Millionaire Success Habits, Totally Fulfilled,* **and** *The Underdog Advantage.*

Preface

In a time when fear, sadness, division, and uncertainty cloud the world, may this book find you and illuminate your path.

Inspire, by Lynee Palacios, is an 11-chapter collection of lifelong learnings about life, love, and everything in between. Each section of this book tackles a different aspect of life, but all are connected inherently and center on the single aim of finding one's purpose and making a difference- by being inspired and being an inspiration.

This is for anyone from any walk of life, especially those who feel lost in their own paths or who are traveling with no destination in sight. Let this book be a source of guidance and inspiration for anyone who has been trying to find their rightful place in the vast sea of life.

Introduction

As an inquisitive person, I've always believed that the purpose of life is to grow as an individual, and through my journey, I realized that this growth is a lifelong process.

Every life has a story and mine starts here...

Growing up as a reserved and shy child, nobody would have pictured me to be the person I am now. As a kid, I felt uncomfortable receiving recognition or acknowledgment and was afraid of the world in general. With this unhealthy diffidence, I faded into the background, unnoticed. I was labeled as weird and different because I was socially awkward and preferred to be on my own, immersed deeply within a book rather than playing like kids my age. I heard the word "weird" so frequently that I felt like it would be ingrained in my identity forever. I perceived this attribute as something negative, and it greatly influenced how I viewed myself for years, and how I navigated my way through adulthood in search of my voice.

Looking back, I can say that these building blocks rooted in my childhood molded me into who I am now as a person and also influenced the aspirations, realities, and relationships I built in life. If I could talk to my younger self, who carried on her neck heavy labels that she couldn't seem to take off, I would let her know that her weirdness and awkwardness were not impediments. Rather, they are key elements of her personhood, ready to unfold, setting her up for a successful and purposeful life. I'd tell her not to put too much pressure on herself and to take each day one step at a time. Her quirks and peculiarities set her apart. I'd encourage her to embrace herself, and trust that there's a path for everyone, even for those who haven't found their voices yet.

Finding My Voice

Unsure of myself and lacking the confidence to speak up, I had always admired people who were comfortable speaking their minds and aspired to be like them. This became my motivation as I started my journey towards adulthood. Knowing that I won't be able to get far in life if I were afraid of socializing or conveying my opinions to others, I tried my best to speak my mind and be more sociable and open, and during the process, I realized that growth happens when we muster the courage to get out of our comfort zones.

My newfound courage guided me as I continued my journey of finding my place in this world. I grew up in a close-knit and very protective family, so moving out at the age of 17 and driving across the country by myself had been quite a tough, yet enriching adventure for me. At first, it was a challenge for me to adjust and detach from my family and the norms that I was used to, but I knew I needed to do that to grow and defy the limits I set for myself.

My Journey Continues

I always believed that the only way for me to feel accomplished and fulfilled was to realize my childhood dream and become an established doctor. With the unending support of my family and the stars aligning for me and my dreams, I was fortunate enough to earn a double major in Physiological Sciences and Human Nutrition at The University of Arizona.

Determined to land in a good place in life, I painstakingly focused on my studies and did my best to keep my grades high throughout my academic years. All of my hard work eventually paid off once I got accepted into medical school.

I can say that I was completely absorbed by my dream, obsessed rather, and oblivious to the truth that the pivotal moment of my life would soon manifest itself. To pay my way through medical school, I had my summer internship as a traveling salesperson. I walked door-to-door selling books and earned just enough to survive as an aspiring adult. I even remember asking what I got myself into and felt like I was a complete mess during the first few weeks of independence and adult life. I was unaware that this particular phase would become the turning point in my life. During this stage, I would gradually come out of my shell and discover my potential in the business industry.

When One Door Closes, Another One Opens

I consider my summer internship as one of the most important events of my life. It helped me recognize my strengths and capitalize on them, opened new doors, improved my confidence, and enhanced my marketing and people skills. It was also during my unforgettable summer internship that my love for knowledge and learning proved itself beneficial. I spent my free time reading and found the greatest treasure through the hundreds of books I'd read. It was a personal development book that would unknowingly change my life forever. It's entitled, ***Unlimited Power,*** which was coincidentally written by Tony Robbins, who, by an amazing turn of events, I would have the honor and pride to work for.

Amused with how Tony's words changed the way I viewed and lived my life, I read other personal development books thereafter. Gradually, I felt like I was looking at life with brand new eyes, and before I knew it, I was already attracting opportunities beyond my imagination. These books made me realize that limitless possibilities are everywhere. We just need the determination to look for them. They also helped me find the courage to take up new challenges in life and not be afraid of the capricious road that lies ahead.

If there's one thing I realized along my adventure, it's that our paths in life remain uncertain. That we will encounter life's surprises and possibilities, whether or not we like it, and it's the same uncertainty that will lead us to the place where we ought to be.

With financial matters affecting my studies in medical school, I decided to put it on hold. I started a meal-prepping business to save and continue with my education. That business ended up doing well and eventually became my primary source of income.

The unpredictability of life left me astounded. I went full force in the entrepreneurial field, and I ended up loving it so much that before I knew it; I was already scaling my business. Just then, another opportunity opened before my eyes. I was offered to work for a company headed by Tony Robbins and Dean Graziosi, the same people to whom I looked up to and had, unbeknownst to them, made tremendous changes in my life. These inspiring and respectable men became a huge inspiration not only to me but to thousands of others whose lives they've touched, and I consider myself fortunate to have met my life's heroes.

To work alongside the greatest life coaches and visionaries of our time is a once-in-a-lifetime opportunity that presented itself when I needed it the most, not just for my professional advancement, but for personal growth as well. So, I took an enormous leap of faith and sold my business. It was one of the hardest decisions that I've ever made, as I considered it an extension of myself. Being a registered dietician and a nutritional guru in my circle, I provided guidance and support to my clients on their journey towards fitness and a healthy lifestyle. But even though I had to let go of my business and start anew, I was given the honor of collaborating with the people I looked up to for years and this paved the way for me to realize what my true calling was.

My True Calling

Being part of the self-development industry and managing a community of 20,000 members, I got to know myself better and discovered my true purpose in life. Looking at Dean Graziosi, Tony Robbins, and all the other inspiring coaches, I was motivated to live my life to the fullest, seize every opportunity that I encountered, and through the process, touch the lives of others and make a difference in the world.

With almost four fruitful years with the Mastermind Community, I realized that my true calling was to inspire others to take action, support them in their growth, and constantly motivate them to become better versions of themselves. I want to become an inspiration to anyone who might be in the same position that I once was - someone weighed down by inescapable labels, or who feels stuck in a phase in life; I aspire to be an instrument in finding the path for anyone who feels lost and in reclaiming the voice of the voiceless.

A New Adventure Awaits

Looking back on all the experiences I've had in life; I can say that my journey has been a culmination of purposeful events and adventures that eventually led me to an uncertain yet promising future.

Over the next few years, I served as the Strategic Manager and Community Director of Mastermind.com, a company that caters to over 20,000 members across the globe and is dedicated to helping people discover their strengths and allow them to see a better path to succeed in life. Being part of this wonderful community has been one of the most meaningful chapters of my life. All the lessons I've gained and the relationships I've built throughout my time there, I'll forever treasure and take with me wherever life's tides take me.

But like any other story, when one chapter ends, another one begins. The year 2020 was a period full of challenges and lessons, triumphs, and defeats. And although I experienced various obstacles, it became a year of personal awakening and realization for me. After almost four years, I knew I was ready to start a new adventure. I courageously left Mastermind.com, which has been my haven, the home that I've searched for as an unsure and self-doubting girl, years ago. I knew in my heart that it was time to carve my own path.

Because of all the things that life has taught me, I can proudly say that I'm ready to see what lies ahead for me on my journey. I want to discover more about myself and explore the possibilities of life. At the moment, I am focusing on my Virtual Assistance Business, VIAA, and my Wonder Women Community that I have established, together with my fellow life and business coaches.

Everything was slowly unfolding, but life has a way of surprising us with its unexpected wonders. It was in May 2021, a year when the world was filled with chaos and uncertainty, that I found my source of peace. I was given the greatest blessing of my life as I was able to bring forth a beautiful, unparalleled, and sacred life into the world. I became a mother to my precious baby, Charlee.

I may have millions of questions left unanswered, but now I see that all the decisions and steps I took in life led me to this moment. And along this uncertain and winding journey, I have grown into the woman I was meant to be.

I know you've been waiting for your break, your moment, just like I once did. And although it may take us an eternity to find our place, I promise you, it'll all be worth it. So, hold on to your dreams and in due time, you'll be off to do bigger and better things. In a few short years, you'll say goodbye to everything that's been keeping you in doubt; and hello to the rest of your life. I am so excited to see all the amazing things you'll do, and the breathtaking places you'll go. But wherever life takes you, I hope you remember to live fully and enjoy every second of the moment you're in.

And with every moment of your life, I want you to seize every opportunity with conviction, for these opportunities are a culmination of the sacrifices that you make to achieve your goals. They are the possibilities that you create for yourself.

Let this book be a source of guidance and inspiration for anyone who has been trying to find a place or a voice. I encourage you to continue to solve the mystery of your shyness or your flaws and to see them not as an enemy, but as a guide and motivator. You have the ability to surpass all the limits you set for yourself, which will help you and many others.

I encourage you to stand and to speak with those interested in your knowledge. I encourage you to share your story with others, know that you're worthy, and strive to be an inspiration. And even though the solution to the riddle of life appears elusive, I promise you that one day you'll look at this particular phase in your life, with a smile, and realize that it was not the destination that matters, it was the journey and the growth that goes with it that made life worth living.

So, are you ready to start your journey towards transcendence and transformation? Come join me as we defy all the limits and doubts, let's embrace authenticity, and discover the limitless possibilities of life.

With love,

Lynee Palacios

Author's Note

This, for me, is more than just a book. It's a guide and an invitation toward understanding and striving for a more purposeful life. It's a collection of my lifelong discoveries, reflections, lessons, and experiences. I encourage you to treat this as a gift and use it well.

"Inspire," is divided into 11 chapters, each intended for a particular aspect of life. You can start at any chapter of this book that you prefer or deem the most beneficial for your present situation. Finish one chapter, including the exercises at the end of each before moving onto the next one.

Before you embark on this journey, I want you to look for a sanctuary in your house or anywhere you feel at ease and comfortable. You'll be needing this to accomplish some of the challenges for the action part at the end of each chapter.

So, with that, let's get started!

Chapter 1

Success Is a Mindset

"The greatest discovery of all time is that a person can change his future by merely changing his attitude."
– Oprah Winfrey

Your mindset is invaluable. It influences the course of your journey and even your ultimate destination in life. With its powerful force, it can either drive or prevent you from reaching your full potential. When harnessed correctly, mindset becomes one of the strongest tools that you can have in your inventory.

My journey as an independent and self-driven person didn't happen overnight. Growing up in a simple household, my parents were earning just enough money to provide for our daily needs. At that age, I knew that with our condition, we wouldn't be able to afford my college fees. So, I decided to work and use my earnings to provide for my education. Lacking confidence and conviction, there were times when I wanted to give up. But the thought of helping my family and making them proud always fueled me to try again. Amidst the challenges life threw at me, I realized that success includes getting lost along the way but having the courage and perseverance to get back up and build your new path. I used some of the most cathartic and painful points of my life as my motivation to create my own success, and this was when I understood that success is something that you have to define for yourself; and having a healthy and positive mindset will lead you to the success you've dreamed of.

Pause and think about the belief that's been playing in your head as you live your daily life. Remarks such as, "I can't do this," "I'm not good enough," "I can't cope with the demands of life," or "I'm not worthy." These are the thoughts subconsciously stuck on replay in your mind. They are the voices that seem impossible to silence, gradually eating your confidence and reinforcing your self-doubts and inhibitions.

These statements and opinions are what we call self-limiting beliefs. To put it simply, they are negative personal assumptions or perceptions that are rooted in your past experiences. They affect how you view yourself, the situation you're in, and life in general. These assumptions are "self-limiting" because, in one way or another, they're holding you back from achieving your full potential.

Whether it is conscious or unconscious, these narratives become your truth. They become the gospel that your mind believes in. But ask yourself this: Where did these beliefs come from? Who made you believe these things are your truth? If your beliefs have this powerful influence on your end results, can you imagine how much more potential you could create and what you could accomplish, if every belief you had completely sustained, supported, and nurtured you instead?

By going through this quick journey with me, I want you to know how powerful the mind is, and with your trust, I aspire to bring out the hidden potentials you've been unknowingly concealing. You hold the key to your success. You are the author of your destiny!

> *"Success is a mindset. Let's learn how to create a positive one."*
> **-Beau Norton**

Change Your Thoughts to Change Your Life

The human mind is indeed fascinating. It is limitless as it needs to be. Your brain, the mind's physical counterpart, generates about 12-25 watts of electricity, which is enough to power a low-wattage light bulb! It possesses its own patterns, unique tendencies, and special mechanisms. It is indeed magnificent and the possibilities that it can create are boundless.

The beauty of the human mind is outstanding.

According to an article made by the National Science Foundation (2005) on human thoughts, an average person has between 12,000 to 60,000 thoughts per day. Of those thoughts, 80% are considered negative and 95% are repetitive thoughts.

It's noteworthy that with this amount of information, if you take time and write all the thoughts passing through your minds, you could write a book each day! But the question is, would it be a book you'd be proud of? It appears that most of your creations would be a book based on your worries, fears, regrets, and complaints about yourself, with only a few positive chapters.

Let's change those statistics! Let's increase the positive thoughts. Remember that what you focus on gets bigger. You become what you believe! And even when it seems impossible to look on the bright side of things, it's actually 100% in your power to transform the way you see life.

Cultivating Success Mindset

We all yearn for success and happiness in our lives, and no matter how grand or humble our dreams in life are, we must embrace the idea that "success is a mindset," and try our best to foster and cultivate a frame of mind that creates this success.

You've probably been asked before whether you're a "glass-half-full," or a "glass-half-empty," kind of person, and you might be unaware that this is a way of looking at one's mindset- a powerful tool from which your mental attitude, inclination towards a goal, and principles in life are founded on, and that which determines how you view the world and form your decisions.

Before you start with your journey towards a success mindset, it's important to clarify that the definition of success is personal or subjective. Some consider money and power the most important criteria of success, while others look at deeper factors such as the quality of the relationships someone possesses, one's mental stability, or the level of happiness that one feels, as the ultimate measurement of success.

Although it is viewed differently, I, for one, believe that success is not a single action that you take. Rather, it's a way of life, a frame of mind- a mindset! And it is important to acknowledge that if you want to accomplish great things in life, you must also reflect greatness in everything that you do.

Thus, whatever you want to accomplish on this big journey, your path to success only begins when you adopt the right mindset.

The Three Facets of a Success Mindset

"Whatever the mind can conceive and believe, it can achieve."
- **Napoleon Hill**

The most beautiful aspect of life is that you are allowed to create your reality in every moment of your existence. You can construct your future with every single thought. This becomes a fundamental key to your success. If you want to change your life and empower yourself to create an amazing future, then you must acknowledge that you are the author of your own story. You hold the pen to your future, and you alone can make the decision of transforming your life.

We've all seen people do it. We've long been an audience of successful leaders, celebrities, entrepreneurs, and all other accomplished figures from any field of expertise. Looking at their practice and keys to success, we can see a common trend, they all possess their own thought process or belief system called success mindset.

In this chapter, we'll be going through the three things that define the success mindset:

I. Success Mentality Utilizes the Growth Mindset

Carol Dweck, an American psychologist and a pioneer researcher in the field of motivation, described in her book, "Mindset: The New Psychology of Success," the two different mindsets that can affect how we navigate our lives: The fixed and growth mindset.

Fixed Vs. Growth Mindset

The crucial difference between fixed and growth mindset is in the belief that intelligence and abilities are permanent or temporary. One considers it as permanent with no room for change or improvement, while the other views it as changeable, with opportunities for growth, advancement, and improvement.

A growth mindset is where one views intelligence and abilities as things that can be developed or harnessed. Here, we believe we can be better, wiser and strive to cultivate more skills and abilities by investing our time and effort into it. A fixed mindset, on the other hand, assumes that abilities and intelligence are relatively fixed and permanent. Here, we do not believe that our skills and capabilities can be enhanced. We are governed by the idea that we either have it or we don't when it comes to our talents and abilities.

The difference in mindsets leads to a contrast in behavior and perception of things. Believing that intelligence and abilities are perpetual and inflexible would lead to limiting our effort to improve, while believing that we can improve our abilities would lead us to put more effort and time in achieving our goals.

The Benefits of Having a Growth Mindset:

♡ **It strengthens your self-esteem**

We consider a growth mindset the secret to positive self-esteem. Using this healthier approach, you'll be able to view perseverance and effort as your key to success. A growth mindset regards experiencing failures and trials as an opportunity for learning and improvement. It further leads to positive higher confidence, motivation, and resilience, which are valuable for success.

♡ **It builds your abilities and values**

Your way of thinking affects both your abilities and values. Having a growth mindset makes you see the possibility of acquiring new skills and enhancing the ones you already have. It also enables you to see yourself as a work in progress and be motivated to continue improving and aspiring.

♡   **It allows you to understand your strengths and capitalize on them**

Your strengths grow from your skills, talents, patterns of thought, and behavior. Cultivating or enhancing your strengths requires perseverance and motivation, but without a growth mindset, you won't be able to acknowledge and enhance your strength and capitalize on them on our way to success.

♡   **It improves your communication skills**

Your mindset can support or hinder your ability to convey your thoughts. Having feedback as one of the primary tools in developing communication skills, it is only with a growth mindset that you can improve your communication skills. Because with a growth mindset, you'll be more open to criticisms, you can embrace challenges more openly, and you can welcome feedback as an opportunity to improve and learn.

♡   **It allows creating a compelling and inspiring vision**

We describe visions as mental images of potential and a desirable future. They show your aspirations and desired destination in the future. They are equated to your dreams and provide direction in your life. Once they are defined, they become your internal compass that guides your life decisions.

With a growth mindset applied to your goals, you are not just simply following the flow of life, rather, you'll be walking with a rational purpose; You do not accept the idea that you are a victim of your destiny and you stand by the hopes of improvement and growth.

"You are today where your thoughts brought you; you will be tomorrow where your thoughts take you."
-James Allen

II.   It Believes in The Power of Positivity

As you venture into life, you will face obstacles along the way, that's a guarantee. The defining characteristic of people with a success mindset, is their enormous level of positive thought.

The second facet of a success mindset is believing in the positive possibilities of life. This is not blind optimism and doesn't equate to you being in denial of the current situation you're in. What it does is empower you to rule over your situation, realize that you're in charge, and allow you to look for feasible ways to overcome any obstacle you may face.

Genuine optimism shouldn't also be mistaken with toxic positivity. While optimism uses a realistic approach without minimizing one's own or another's emotions, toxic positivity is blindly asserting that everything is good even if it isn't and during the process, discredits and invalidates all other emotions that are not positive. Genuine optimism comes from an authentic belief in yourself and your abilities.

An optimistic view of life is linked to various benefits, including lower stress levels, better coping skills, improved physical and mental health, and increased persistence in reaching a goal.

If you employ a positive mindset in life, you'd view obstacles and challenges as learning experiences or temporary setbacks. That even the most miserable day is an opportunity to be better.

"The mind has a powerful way of attracting things that are in harmony with it, good and bad."
- Idowu Koyenikan

III. It Acknowledges the Importance of Self-Awareness

Success starts with mastering your inner propensities and determining what you excel at. With this, you can find your niche and live a life of purpose.

Knowing yourself allows you to recognize your strengths, and this gives you a better understanding of the unique qualities that will allow you to reach the goals that you set for yourself. Similarly, it's important to gain insight into your weaknesses to continue to grow and improve.

You also need to be self-aware to understand that you're only human and face both your strengths and weaknesses with maturity. When you develop self-awareness, it makes it easier to take the good with the bad, forgive and learn from your shortcomings, and succeed in life.

> *"Your visions will become clear only when you can look into your own heart. Who looks outside, dreams; who looks inside, awakes."*
> *- C.G. Jung*

Take Action!

This 1st Challenge will help you reframe aimless, negative thoughts, retrain your mind to create alternative paths, shift your perspective, and help you see things with brand new eyes. Follow the step-by-step action plan and create your very own success mindset!

1. Close your eyes and reflect on all the things you wish to change in your life. All your fears, your doubts, and inhibitions. The things that have been keeping you from achieving your potential. Stop, pause for a while, and focus on your breathing. As you inhale and exhale, remind yourself that while this is a tough moment, sacrifices and difficulties are a part of life. Create soothing phrases that are personal and meaningful to you, such as "I accept myself as I am," "With my determination, I can get

through this, and learn from the setbacks that I encounter," or "I forgive myself for all my imperfections, just as I would forgive others."

2. Create your gratitude journal. Take 15 minutes each day and write five things for which you feel grateful.
3. Take a moment and envision your ideal future. Write what it looks like and imagine yourself reaching that goal. Now, list down 3 virtues that you need in order to achieve your purpose.
4. Be accountable and execute this first challenge for a week. On the 7th day, reflect on the changes that the challenge has brought to your life.

"Twenty years from now, you will be more disappointed by the things you didn't do than by the ones you did. So throw off the bowlines. Sail away from the safe harbor. Catch the trade winds in your sails. Explore. Dream. Discover."
–Mark Twain

Lynee Palacios

Chapter 2

Connecting The Body & The Mind

"Every sacred soul has a sacred body."
- Lailah Gifty Akita

A clear distinction is frequently made between the body and the mind. But when talking about holistic well-being, mental and physical health should not be thought of as separate entities, for a strong link exists between your mental and physical wellness. Indeed, a serene mind is nothing without a healthy body to carry it, and vice versa.

It has always been my dream to author a book on nutrition, which is my expertise; However, with everything that the world is facing at present, I felt like I needed to share more. I consider it a calling to inspire others to strive for a balanced life. To constantly look for steadiness and equilibrium in all aspects of existence, such as health, love, and relationships. The fragility of life has been revealed to us over the past few years. So, we need to live every moment of our borrowed time as meaningful and as balanced as we can.

So, let me ask you: When was the last time you took care of yourself? When did you last focus on what makes you happy and nourished, prioritized your well-being, and made a conscious effort to love and appreciate your authentic self? Through this chapter, I want you to reflect on how you're treating your body and answer this ultimate question: How can you take care of yourself from the inside out so that you can fully experience a meaningful and happy life?

As you step into this new journey with me, I want you to acknowledge that every waking day that you've been given, your body has taken care of you. I want you to reflect on whether you've also done your part in taking care of your body. Often, you might be too consumed by the things around you, your career, your responsibilities, your dreams, or even the people in your life, that you lose focus on yourself.

I want you to understand that your relationship with yourself is the defining factor in shaping the life you aspire to live. For your truth depends on how you love and take care of yourself.

No one is responsible for your health and wellness but yourself, so you must do all you can to keep your health balanced. And it is only when you take care of yourself that you can share your gifts and be an inspiration to others.

Allow me to help you open new doors towards self-discovery and transformation. Your goal now is to love and treat yourself better. Because part of getting the life you want is taking care of your body and mind.

"Nourishing yourself in a way that helps you blossom in the direction you want to go is attainable, and you are worth the effort."
– Deborah Day

Connecting The Body and The Mind

The perceived disconnection between the body and the mind creates the misconception that mental and physical well-being aren't directly related. In reality, your mental health has a direct impact on your physical health, and similarly, your physical state affects your mental well-being in ways you may not be aware of. Given the right care, your mind and body become the most powerful allies that you can use in attaining your goals in life.

By acknowledging the connection between your body and mind, you'll be able to refuel your physical and mental energies, which will create peace from within, remind you who you really are, and allow you to visualize your goals in life. With this balance, you'll be able to have a purposeful existence that will allow you to make a difference in the world.

Your physical, psychological, and mental wellness are all essential to a healthy and fulfilling life. Now, your goal is to allow all these essential factors to thrive in unison by equally cultivating them, and the key lies in finding a balance for both the body and the mind. The challenge, however, is in finding the techniques that would allow you to do so.

So, let me take you to a road that will lead you to a balanced and holistically healthy life, one that you rightfully deserve.

Listen To Your Body, Strengthen Your Mind

"Your body is your vehicle for life. As long as you are here, live in it. Love, honor, respect and cherish it, treat it well, and it will serve you in kind."
- Suzy Prudden

Balance is perceived differently, for each of us carries different levels of tolerance for incongruence, holds varied needs for balance in the different areas of our lives, and possesses different resources for achieving stability.

With all the setbacks that you may encounter along your journey, you may find yourself living a stress-driven and exhausting kind of life, and as you are in a constant hurry to achieve various goals and find your place in this world, you may fail to realize that your body is already in protest and demands you to pay attention to its needs. Your body and mind deserve some rest.

Now's the time to listen to what your body's telling you and attend to what your mind is imparting.

So, How Can You Listen to Your Body?

Listening to your body means being attentive to all the messages it uses to convey its needs. Essentially, it's giving your body the vital things and treatment that it deserves, like food for nourishment, movement for fitness, or rest to replenish your energy.

These are some ways to listen to what your body is telling you:

1. **Respect your body and mind**

   Respecting the body and mind means respecting and honoring it. It's treating your body with the same care you would bestow upon anything of value to you. Acts that show respect to your body and mind include:

♡ Complimenting yourself- Appreciate your strengths and remind yourself of your potential

♡ Never compare yourself to others- Unhealthy comparison breeds negative feelings such as envy, and low self-confidence it also compromises your ability to trust others. Remember: Every minute spent comparing your path to someone else's is a minute lost in creating your own.

♡ Wear comfortable clothes- Feeling comfortable in your clothes allows you to listen to what your body needs, without being distracted or feeling out of breath. Enjoying movement is also easier when you aren't distracted by your clothes. Throwing out old clothes is also considered a cathartic experience- especially when it's associated with healthy dieting.

Whenever you respect your body and mind, you become grounded in both the physical and mental aspects of your life. This type of respect carries reciprocal energy, that goes: Your body and mind will honor you when you honor them.

"When you start loving yourself and respecting your time and energy, things will change. Get to know your worth, and your value will go up."
– **Germany Kent**

2. Be active and exercise!

Being physically active is great for managing your physical health, as well as improving your mental well-being. As exercise affects the uptake of feel-good chemicals in the brain such as endorphins, it is considered a natural way of increasing energy, reducing stress, and keeping your body healthy.

Moving your body is one of the most beneficial things that you can do for your mind. Physically active people are happier and more satisfied with their lives. They have a stronger sense of purpose and experience more happiness, hope, and courage. They feel more connected to their communities and are less likely to suffer from loneliness or depression.

Physical activities and exercises of any form will go a long way in reducing stress, especially if it's done right. Even just a brisk walk in the morning will make you feel energized and motivated for the day ahead.

"An early morning walk is a blessing for the whole day."
— Henry David Thoreau

3. **Make sleep and rest your priority**

Sleep plays a vital role in protecting your immune system and assisting brain functions. Healthy sleep improves your ability to learn new information and form memories. It also helps in restoring neural connections, assists in emotional control, social interaction, and decision making.

The advisable amount of sleep for each person may vary, but generally, an adult should get 7-9 hours of sleep per night. Creating your own routine or schedule of getting adequate sleep is one of the most effective ways towards mental wellness. Your body should be your best friend. Give it the rest and sleep that it deserves.

"Each night, when I go to sleep, I die. And the next morning, when I wake up, I'm reborn."
– Mahatma Gandhi

4. **Balance your diet**

Food is fuel for the body, and it's essential in functioning optimally in life. Your food intake influences the way you feel about yourself, the situation you're in, or even life in general. A balanced diet includes a healthy amount of essential fats, vitamins, minerals, proteins, complex carbohydrates, and water.

Your everyday nutrition influences your growth and aids in the prevention and treatment of physical and mental health conditions. Without balance in your food intake, your body will be more prone to diseases.

Tips for a balanced diet:

✓ Create an eating plan for each week- this will be the key to a fast and easy healthy meal preparation.

✓ Prepare most of your meals at home using whole and minimally processed foods.

✓ Eat healthy food by focusing on fruits and vegetables that will nourish your body with a wide variety of vitamins and minerals. Fill half your plate with vegetables and fruit for every meal. Choose brightly colored fruits and vegetables, especially orange and dark green vegetables. Canned or frozen, unsweetened fruits and vegetables would be a perfect alternative to fresh ones.

✓ Avoid sugary drinks such as juices and sodas, and instead, hydrate yourself by drinking plenty of water (8-12 glasses a day). Low-fat, unsweetened milk is also a good option to stay hydrated. Keep a reusable water bottle with you wherever you go, so you can stay hydrated throughout the day.

✓ Choose whole-grain food instead of refined and processed grains, for they contain fiber, B vitamins, and protein to help you stay healthy and full longer. Whole grain food includes crackers and bread, hulled barley, and oatmeal, which are produced from whole grains.

✓ Eat Proteins that help build and maintain strong bones, skin, and muscles. Proteins can come from nuts, seeds, fish, eggs, milk (low fat), legumes, tofu, yogurt (low fat), kefir (low fat), and cheese.

✓ Limit highly processed food intake. These are foods that are changed from their original source and have been mixed with various ingredients. During the process, important nutrients such as fiber, vitamins, and minerals are removed while sugar and salt are added. Highly processed food includes fast foods and snacks such as chips, cookies, hot dogs, frozen pizza, white rice, and bread, among others.

✓ Avoid too many sweets because it can lead to unhealthy weight gain, problems in your blood sugar, and an increased risk of heart disease, among other dangerous conditions. Because of this, added sugar should be kept to a minimum level, which is easy when you follow a healthy diet based on whole foods.

✓ Eat smaller meals more often. Eat at least three meals a day with snacks in between. When you wait too long to eat, you'll be more likely to make unhealthy food choices. Keep healthy, easy-to-eat snacks.

"One must eat to live, not live to eat."
- Jean-Baptiste Poquelin

5. Schedule a quick morning meditation

Doing a five to ten-minute meditation each morning will help in balancing and preparing your mind and body for the busy day ahead. Take a few moments to relax before you begin your day. Think about all the things you are grateful for; your life, your work, or even the fact that you are given another day to live and to be with the people you love. Let go of everything that's holding you back and take just a small part of your time to be thankful for every opportunity that may come to you.

"The more regularly and the more deeply you meditate, the sooner you will find yourself always acting from a center of peace."
– J. Donald Walters

6. Slow down, Pause, and Breathe

It's easy for you to get caught up in a continuous cycle of work, sleep, and more work. Life moves so fast that it seems to pass you before you can truly enjoy it; However, it doesn't have to be this way. I want you to fight against a hectic lifestyle and slow down to enjoy your life. This slowing down is a conscious choice that you can freely make, but not necessarily an easy one. You have to understand that slowing down and pausing in life leads to a greater appreciation of your existence and a greater level of happiness.

Set a reminder on your calendar, or perhaps an alarm on your phone, anything to push you, so that amid your busy day, you'll allow yourself to step back and check in with yourself by asking and answering honestly how you're feeling. And whatever emotions you're perceiving, know that it's valid. Acknowledge and explore it without judgment.

When you find yourself in a fast-paced cycle and stressing out, I want you to pause and take a deep breath. Take a couple more. Consciously feel the air coming in and out of your body and along with the air, you'll feel the stress also moving out. By focusing on each breath, you'll be bringing yourself back to the present. Do this every day to show your body the same love and compassion you freely give to others. You deserve it!

> **".Nature does not hurry, yet everything is accomplished."**
> **- Lao Tzu**

Take Action!

This next challenge is for you to open the door towards self-love, appreciation, gratitude, and willingness. Reflect and answer the following question:

1. List three words that come into mind when you think of the word "Self-love"
2. Name three things you love about your body.
3. Write a letter apologizing to your body for ways you may have neglected, mistreated, or spoken badly about it. Be gentle with yourself while reflecting on your shortcomings. After writing your short letter of apology, situate yourself in front of a mirror and say this phrase to yourself:

   "After years of abusing and neglecting you, I am now finally learning to love you and respect you for all that you have done and all that you will continue to do for me. From now on, I will treat you right, simply because that's what you deserve."

4. After finishing the challenge, I want you to reflect on the changes that the task has brought you.

There are approximately 7.8 billion people in the entire world, but there's only one precious individual with whom you'll always be in a relationship, for the rest of your life, and that's yourself. But because it is only by being kind to both your body and mind, can you live your life at peace with every piece of you, I want to encourage you to start being a good companion to yourself. Be your own best friend! Now's the time to acknowledge what your body has already done and will continue to do for you. Appreciate, respect, and cherish yourself. You are worthy! You are a work of art!

"And I said to my body softly, 'I want to be your friend.' It took a long breath and replied, 'I've been waiting my whole life for this.'"
- Nayyirah Waheed

Chapter 3

The Value of Spiritual Wellness

"Believe in your infinite potential. Your only limitations are those you set upon yourself."
- Roy T. Bennett

Spiritual wellness is an integral part of the physical, mental, and psychological health of man. It is considered the backbone of wellness, for it affects all the other components of your well-being, and with the absence of a strong spiritual connection, every other aspect of wellness cannot reach its full potential. It is one of the primary resources that you can use on your journey towards recovery and healing. So, just as you continuously strive to balance your physical and mental wellness, you should never neglect the spiritual element of your health.

It's an honor to share with you my spiritual journey, which has given me immense purpose and inspiration, molded me to be the person I am today, and made me realize that our lives are significant in a complex way beyond our mundane everyday existence. At the age of 18, I started questioning my deepest "why's" in life. I've always been interested and curious about Religion. I came from a religiously conservative family, but my curiosity allowed me to uncover a life I never dreamed possible. As I was in the process of knowing myself and understanding life, I explored other religions that all handed me a piece of the puzzle that I've tried completing as an unsure girl. Through this exploration, I started becoming more self-aware, intuitive, authentic, and unconditional.

This intimate quest for a deeper insight of life has been one of my purposes for authoring my first book. We are living in the most unprecedented times; without a deeper purpose or an ultimate reason to live, we may find ourselves feeling lost and dreading every step we're about to take. May your journey with me, through this book, be an instrument that'll allow you to discover a life of purpose and meaning, find fulfillment, increase your joy and peace, and grow your spiritual life.

This is my invitation to you, to reflect on whether you're truly living your life, to appreciate the mysteries that go with it, and to know that there's a greater force - bigger than you or anything you've ever known – where you can rest your worries and fears. Regardless of how you express your spirituality, your practice should ultimately be grounded in love, compassion, and realization that you are a significant part of the purposeful unfolding of life.

Viktor Frankl, in his psychological memoir, **Man's Search for Meaning**, stated that man's deepest desire is to search for meaning and purpose. Life then becomes meaningful to people when they can find answers to the vital questions about life, such as: **Who am I? Why am I here? What gives me hope and meaning? What is important to me? Where can I find comfort in this world? And what am I supposed to do with my life?**

Through this journey, I want you to discover a life of purpose and meaning, to find fulfillment, increase your joy and peace, and grow your spiritual life. This is my invitation to you, to reflect on whether you're truly living your life, to appreciate the mysteries that go with it, and to know that there's a greater force, bigger than you, or anything you've ever known, where you can rest your worries and fears.

To live a meaningful and purposeful life, one must take care of all the aspects of wellness, the mind, body, and spirit. Come with me, and let's explore the spiritual element of your life, for without it, you will miss a vital piece of your recovery puzzle.

"He who has a 'why' to live, can bear with almost any 'how'."
- Friedrich Nietzsche

So, what is Spiritual Wellness?

Spiritual wellness refers to the attribute of being connected to something greater than yourself and having a set of values, morals, principles, and beliefs that provide you a clear sense of purpose and meaning in life. This then becomes your compass that will guide your actions. At its core, spirituality is profoundly personal, and you–and only you can define what it means and the role that it has in your life. Your spiritual wellness guides you in making your decisions in life, ground you during periods of change, and gives you resiliency to survive when faced with adversity.

Spiritual wellness encompasses everything from your daily discipline to finding your true purpose in life. It is a culmination of the values and beliefs which a person lives by. Implementing realistic standards and boundaries based on your beliefs and values is crucial because without them it is next to impossible to find your calling and reach your full potential. Spirituality is necessary to attain fulfillment.

In understanding spiritual wellness better, a good starting point is to consider the premise that man's deepest desire in life is to search for meaning and purpose. For anyone who may be feeling a growing sense of loss, or uncertainty, as life progresses, possessing a strong connection with your spirituality can make a difference in your inner peace and sense of fulfillment. Thus, the person you become results from an inner decision and not one merely of outside influences. Holding on to your morals and spirituality turns any experience, no matter how difficult, into a triumphant story.

Various factors play a part in defining spiritual health – religious beliefs, faith, ethics, principles, values, and morals. Some also gain spirituality by cultivating personal relationships with others, or by being at peace with nature. Although the understanding of spiritual health is different for each person, the only constant thing about spirituality is that it allows you to find the inner calm and peace needed to get through life and live for a greater purpose. So, no matter what your beliefs are, or where you may be on your spiritual journey, the basis of spirituality is discovering a sense of meaning and knowing that you have a purpose to fulfill.

In totality, spiritual wellness means contemplating your purpose in life and achieving total awareness and mindfulness of your impact on the rest of the world

"You need tremendous spirituality to stop yourself
from falling into the abyss."
-Ingrid Betancourt

Finding Your "Why" in Life

Have you ever wondered what your reasons are for
waking up and living every day?

Finding your why in life is the most powerful thing you
can do for your overall wellness, for without a clear
"why" behind your actions and decisions, your life
becomes filled with confusion and fear, but when you
have clarity of your why's in life, you'll live a life filled
with direction and meaning.

All of us go through life in search of our own "whys."
We are on a constant quest for the purpose of our
existence. We have different roads to take and choices
to make. While some falter and cease in their search,
others succeed in their journey and gain successful
discoveries about themselves and their reasons for
living. Others succeeded in their quest and discovered
their purpose, but still navigated a different path,
pursuing another dream.

You may be on this journey because, like me, you're
also in search of your life's purpose. I salute you for
making it this far, for aspiring to see life with brand
new eyes, and for navigating it with purpose and
meaning. Allow me to guide you on your journey
towards spiritual wellness, and a life well-lived.

*"The two most important days in your life are the day
you are born and the day you find out why."*
– Mark Twain

**So, What Can You Do to Achieve a Spiritually Healthy
Life?**

1. Explore and examine your spiritual core

>Actively searching through life or the act of
>exploring how you can make your life
>meaningful and purposeful, increases your
>options and potential for spiritual centering. By
>asking yourself questions like Who am I? What
>are the things I value in life? What is my purpose
>for living? This will lead you to in-depth
>knowledge about yourself and allow you to
>discover your mission. With this, you'll be able
>to go toward your calling and achieve a
>purposeful life.

>There are various ways of examining and
>exploring your spiritual core. Going on a silent
>retreat or going to a peaceful sanctuary will
>renew your enthusiasm in life. Spending time
>outdoors is one of the best and most effective
>means of connecting with your inner self. You
>can also just take a walk and let your mind
>wander through the beauty that stands before
>you.

"Each of us is born for a purpose, and we want our lives to matter. I don't think it's unique to only some of us; it's a longing of every human being."
- Garrett Gravesen

2. Meditate and Practice Mindfulness

Meditation and Mindfulness both have physical and mental benefits for your body. Your physical and mental states are profoundly intertwined and connected to your spiritual wellness, so by strengthening one aspect of your health, you can benefit others. By practicing mindfulness and meditation, you'll allow your unconscious mind to explore your spiritual aspect. Meditation and Mindfulness are considered as a way of life that brings healing and balance to your daily interactions–both external and internal. They refresh and invigorate your whole being.

One form of meditation that's beneficial for spiritual development is Chakra meditation, which is a practice of focusing on each chakra and restoring the energy that flows through them.

A Closer Look at the 7 Chakras

The entire universe is made up of energy, even your physique or body is no exception. From the building blocks of your life to your collective body systems, all of these are made of energy that when interlinked, produce the human energy field. The ancient meditation practice called Tantra (an inner tradition of Hinduism), postulates that every individual has 7 main energy points in the body. These energy points are called chakras, which is a Sanskrit term that means wheel or disk. These spinning disks of energy should be constantly open and aligned, as they correspond to the nerves, other major organs, and areas of your energetic body, and affect your overall well-being.

Buddhists and Hindus believe that the chakras represent the areas in the body where the spiritual and physical states come together. Every chakra rotates at specific speeds, which determine its frequency and color. The 7 chakras play an important role in the balance and overall health of your body. Connecting with your chakras helps you maintain harmony with your mind, body, and spirit, and allows healing and transformation.

1st Chakra -Muladhara or the Root Chakra (Red)

Located at the base of the spine, the root chakra is responsible for your sense of security and survival stability. It also focuses on your basic needs and grounding.

When balanced, the root chakra makes you feel grounded, strong, centered, and secured.

When imbalanced, it can cause anxiety, fear, poor immune system, and joint and lower back pain.

2nd Chakra- Svadhisthana or the Sacral Chakra (Orange)

The sacral chakra is located just below the navel (the pelvic area) and is focused on relationships, passion, creativity, and sexuality.

When balanced, it makes you feel passionate, joyful, and friendly.

When imbalanced, you may experience sexual difficulties, a lack of inspiration and creativity, uterine or bladder issues, or emotional instability.

3rd Chakra- Solar Plexus/ Manipura or the Navel Chakra (Yellow)

Located just between the ribcage and the navel, the solar plexus connects you to your power, affects your relationship to the world and how you view yourself from within, and inherently governs your actions.

When balanced, it makes you confident, productive, and energized.

When imbalanced, solar plexus causes insecurity, low energy, procrastination, muscle cramps, and digestive issues.

4th Chakra- Anahata or the Heart Chakra (Green)

The heart chakra is located within the heart. It's in the middle of all 7 chakras and unites the two classifications of chakras: Chakras of Matter (lower three) with the Chakras of Spirit (upper three). The heart chakra is your source of connection, love, and emotions.

When balanced, you become spiritually aware, generous givers and recipients of love, forgiving, and able to form emotional connections with others.

When imbalanced, it causes unhealthy bouts of loneliness and hatred, circulation problems, and chest pains.

5th Chakra- Vishuddha or the Throat Chakra (Blue)

Located in the throat, it is responsible for the ability to communicate and speak your truth.

When balanced, you'll be able to listen effectively, communicate constructively, and express your authentic self.

When imbalanced, it can cause social anxiety, suppressed emotions, tension headaches, sore throat, and thyroid issues.

6th Chakra- Ajna or the Third Eye Chakra (Indigo)

Located on the forehead, your third eye is the center of divine wisdom, intuition, and insight into the spirit.

When balanced, it allows you to see the world clearly, have an active imagination, and communicate with the universe.

When imbalanced it causes anxiety and depression, low self-esteem, lack of self-trust, and problems with the pituitary and pineal glands.

7th Chakra- Sahasrara or the Crown Chakra (Violet)

Located right at the top of the head, it is your direct connection to the universe.

When balanced, it allows you to accept and process divine guidance, makes you feel enlightened, open-minded, and one with the universe.

When imbalanced, it can cause emotional distress, confusion, materialism, migraines, and problems with the nervous system.

How To Unblock Your Chakras

There are various techniques you can use to restore the balance of your chakras. By employing these, you'll not only clear the pathways of your energy, but restore balance and harmony in all aspects of your wellness as well, bringing you all the benefits of an open and revitalized life.

- ✓ The first step to unblocking your chakras is through awareness. This includes the acknowledgment of the importance of the chakra system and openness to learning ways of purifying, awakening, and aligning your energy field in the promotion of optimum holistic well-being.
- ✓ Consciousness on the physical symptoms that will emerge in the location of a blocked chakra is also vital in unblocking it.
- ✓ Use a mantra or a short repetition of a word or sound to aid concentration in meditation. That is often used at the end of yoga practice and acts as a form of healing that can restore your energy fields.
- ✓ Taking deep breaths with a genuine intention is very effective in restoring your chakras to their natural harmonious state. As you inhale, direct your energy to the identified blocked chakra. As you exhale, focus on relaxing and feel the chakra being unblocked.

"There is deep wisdom within our very flesh if
we can only come to our senses and feel it."
- Elizabeth A. Behnke

3. Take time to reflect

Allotting time for self-reflection is a great way to build self-awareness and improve your spiritual wellness.

By constantly asking yourself questions on your meaning and purpose, goals in life, the difference you want to make, the values you hold in life; You will not only positively affect your holistic health, it will also allow you to carry your purpose and make a difference.

> *"Without reflection, we go blindly on our way, creating more unintended consequences, and failing to achieve anything useful."*
> - Margaret J. Wheatley

4. Increase self-compassion

Self-compassion includes being gentle and discerning toward yourself, especially when faced with hardship or struggles, and involves accepting that failure and suffering are part of the human experience and that all people, including yourself, are worthy of compassion. Self-compassion is also a great motivator for spiritual well-being because it influences the desire to work towards one's purpose, undeterred, alleviate one's suffering, heal and thrive, and make a difference in this world.

By turning your inner critic into your inner coach, you'll perceive setbacks as learning opportunities, be less self-critical, and be able to achieve and give more.

"When you are compassionate with yourself, you trust your soul, which you will let guide your life. Your soul knows the geography of your destiny better than you do"
- John O'Donohue

5. **Cultivate a healthy connection with yourself, with others, or with a higher power (God, Mother Earth, the Universe, Nature, Energy)**

As you continue through your life, the desire to live a spiritual existence proves itself to be essential, and by fostering healthy relationships with yourself, with others, or with a force greater than you, your spiritual health will be nurtured. Spiritual wellness involves a genuine connection and harmony with yourself and the magnificence of the universe. You need to explore what you believe is your own sense of meaning and purpose.

Having healthy connections with yourself, with others, or with a greater force increases your happiness, makes you emotionally healthy, cultivates kindness, and relieves stress. Taking good care of these connections- whether through the relationship you maintain with a higher being or by connecting with others, the choice rests in your hands. Having these healthy relationships offers you something to trust in, a standard to which you can aspire.

Each individual follows a different spiritual path. Faith and spirituality contribute to your sense of oneness, which is a necessary prerequisite for living a holistically healthy life. Only when you see others as an extension of yourself can you build a healthy relationship. And by believing in a transcendent higher purpose, you'll have something in your life that will act as a guiding light and bring inner peace and stability.

I consider my spiritual journey to be something intimate and personal. But sharing this experience in the hope of inspiring others to strive for a healthier spiritual wellness, is an opportunity I'll willingly take.

As a child, I constantly struggled with communicating and speaking my mind. I was wrapped in fear and hesitation, often doubting myself and my value as a person. On my way to conquer my limits and understand my purpose, I realized this fear and inhibition stemmed from an imbalanced chakra. I give equal value to all seven chakras, but found the throat and heart as the two most applicable ones in my life. The throat chakra, given my fear of voicing my opinions, was the most challenging when I was growing up. The heart chakra, being responsible for my longing for love and commitment, also tested me as an adult.

So, how was I able to let go of my fears and accept the love I longed for and rightfully deserved?

I believe that the throat and heart chakra go hand-in-hand. So, before I was able to speak my truth and use my voice to inspire, I first learned to love my authentic self, accepted my whole being and let go of all the hate and fear that had encased me for years.

As I learned more about the chakras, and the ways to balance them, I was able to feel more relaxed, grounded, and in tune with the world. It was then that I felt a harmonious flow of energy within me. I now find myself giving and accepting love that is grounded in honesty, respect, and healthy communication. Finding peace within myself and gaining balance in all the chakras allowed me to be inspired and to live my dream of helping others find their voice.

Take Action!

This challenge will help you find your core, strengthen your spiritual health, and allow you to live a life of meaning and purpose.

1. Reflection is the foundation of spirituality. Look for your personal sanctuary; a place where you can feel relaxed. Go to your chosen haven early in the morning or late in the afternoon. Take a

moment to assess your spiritual wellness by asking yourself the following questions:

What gives your life meaning and purpose?
What gives you hope?
How do you get through tough times?
Where can you find comfort?

2. Fit some quiet time into your daily routine (10–15 minutes after every 2 hours of a busy day) to recharge your inner battery. Use this to observe the present moment, pray or read something that would uplift your soul.

3. Surround yourself with people and things that bring joy, motivation, and tranquility to you.

4. Before going to sleep, sit comfortably and close your eyes. Reflecting on how your day went and what you want to accomplish for the day to come, you can also journal your emotions and/or the lessons you've learned throughout the day, and what will be your concrete plan for you to have a purposeful tomorrow.

5. Be accountable and execute this first challenge for a week. On the 8th day, reflect on the changes that the challenge has brought to your life. Continue the challenge until it becomes a habit.

"A balanced inner calmness radiates from a peaceful center. It neither craves others' approval nor rejects others' presence. It neither pulls towards nor pushes away. It has a reverent attitude towards life and all its inhabitants."
– **Donna Goddard**

Lynee Palacios

Chapter 4

The Beauty of Love

"Love is invisible; yet, it's a very beautiful experience for those who know the true value of it."
- Edmond Mbiaka

Love is beautiful, and its beauty comes from its imperfect nature. It's a mysterious yet powerful force that either binds or divides the world. Love is the source of our strength and vulnerability, unity and discord, hope and despair. It's an enigmatic energy, so strong that it empowers us to accomplish even the things we think are impossible and surpasses all the limits that come our way. Love is, without doubt, the best feeling we can perceive.

You are born with an infinite amount of love within yourself, and through this, you can share and receive it without limit as well. You can give love to anyone, especially those who forgot where to find it. It's beauty is incomparable, for it always stays, it never leaves. And no matter what language you speak, or where you are from, love is an experience and expression that anyone can understand. But for something so universal, its complexity and ambiguity may make it hard to be defined.

The beauty of love has always amazed me. I consider it the most powerful feeling that we can experience. Being inherently ambiguous and complex, this topic has always fascinated me. I have various perceptions about love that were influenced by the different people I met along the way, who, in one way or another, made a difference in my life.

My family, who've been my source of strength, showed me that love is a space for refuge, belongingness, and acceptance.

My precious friends taught me that love understands and accepts differences.

My mentors and those who have influenced me immensely showed me that love is finding your passion, making a difference, and inspiring others.

My partner and my biggest motivator, Jerome, taught me that love is something worth the wait. Love shouldn't be a complication in life, nor a source of agony. Love should be harmonious, accepting, and understanding. It should be easy. It's as natural as breathing. It's simple, effortless, and comfortable. It's an everyday decision of choosing to accept, trust, and respect each other. Love is ultimately the safest place to rest in a tiring world.

Lastly, my daughter taught me that love is selfless and unconditional. It's about making sacrifices and is an indestructible bond so humbling yet so empowering that brings out the strength you never knew you had and the courage you never knew existed.

Love has many definitions and all are the products of our human and personal experiences through every avenue in our journey of life.

So, What Is Love for You?

Each one of us, from every walk of life, has our own interpretation of love, molded from our personal stories and experiences. Being of limitless ability, love is ever changing. It continuously grows and evolves. Love takes various forms and serves numerous purposes. In this chapter, we will look into the different facets of love.

♡ **Love is a basic human need**

Maslow's Hierarchy of Needs characterized love, together with belongingness, as one of the psychological needs of man. It encompasses an immeasurable level of intimacy involving feelings of empathy, compassion, and care, and results in the fulfillment of the sense of belonging and approval. Without the realization of love, you cannot reach self-actualization and you won't be motivated to achieve any goal in life.

Love is the crowning grace of humanity, the holiest right of the soul, the golden link which binds us to duty and truth, the redeeming principle that chiefly reconciles the heart to life, and is prophetic of eternal good.
- Francesco Petrarca

♡ **Love is bigger than us**

Being one of the most benevolent emotions that you can feel; love encompasses varying degrees of both negative and positive emotions, from your most predominant virtues, to your simplest fulfillment. It is where many of your other emotions breed from and is the prime feeling that influences you deeply. With its presence, it develops an additional dimension in your life. Without it, life will feel empty, for love is the force that brings about unity, harmony, and happiness.

"I believe there are some things in life you can't deny or rationalize, and love is one of them."
– Cate Blanchett

♡ Love starts from within

Discovering the true meaning of love and how to experience it fully is a life purpose. It is worth searching for, and through this journey I want you to acknowledge that genuine love starts, first and foremost, from within.

As human beings, it's inevitable to view love as a strong indication of one's worth. And as you search for this validation, you'll find yourself waiting for someone who can fill the void and give you love. But during the process, you may forget about the one person you need to love first-yourself.

Through this chapter, I want you to focus on loving the person in the mirror, understand that you are good enough, that you matter, and that the world is better with you in it. You have a purpose and you are worthy of love. Now's the time for you to see that true love exists and it comes from within. It starts with you. The love you constantly look for comes to you abundantly, only when you realize that you are already whole and complete, and you aren't meant to look for someone who will make you whole again. You are created to embrace your wholeness, and from that, you share your completeness with others. Love flows through you and it ends in you.

What does self-love mean to you?

Each person has a different take on what self-love means and uses varying ways of taking care of themselves. Figuring out what self-love looks like for you as an individual is an important part of your journey towards self-actualization.

Self-love is often interpreted as a state of appreciation for oneself that breeds from actions that support your overall wellness. Self-love means giving importance to your well-being and happiness. It is taking care of your own needs and is the avoidance of sacrificing your well-being just to please others. It is not settling for less than what you deserve.

Another way of looking at self-love is that it is a lifelong commitment. It is a lasting vow with yourself that you will always choose to understand, accept your imperfections, seek the good in every challenge you face, and take care of yourself. Because by loving yourself wholeheartedly, you'll find joy in everything you do and you'll be able to live a life trying to share the love you have within you.

"Love is our most basic human value and also our highest potential."
- Kamand Kojouri

So, How Can You Love Yourself?

✓ **Know yourself.** Your journey towards self-love won't be possible if you don't know who you are, so you need to invest in discovering what your purpose, values, and beliefs are in life. Knowing yourself is a vital step in achieving happiness and peace in life. Daily reflection and meditation can help you in cultivating a deeper understanding of your identity.

✓ **Never compare yourself to others.** The tendency to compare yourself to others is as human as any other emotion. But doing this only makes your life difficult and brings you misery and pain, for it raises feelings of envy, low self-confidence, and discontentment. It also compromises your ability to empathize and trust others. So, instead of comparing yourself to others, try using others as your motivation to work harder and do better. Always keep in mind: Comparison is the thief of joy.

✓ **Acknowledge your achievements, whether big or small.** Success and achievements can have varied meanings to different people, but whether it's accomplishing a goal, overcoming an obstacle, or just merely finding happiness, for you to continue feeling motivated, it's important to celebrate your successes, both big and small. By doing this, you can visualize how far you've traveled, remind yourself of how strong you are, and inspire others when the going gets tough.

✓ **Know your value, say "no" when you need to.** Setting boundaries is an essential form of self-care. It allows you to convey to the world how you want to be treated. Realizing that you are valuable and choosing your own opinion about yourself over others is a brave act that affects your well-being.

✓ **Forgive yourself.** Striving for peace and moving forward is one of the main goals of achieving self-love. By Forgiving yourself for your shortcomings, your flaws, or your fears, you can live a life without feeling pressured and unmotivated. Forgiving refers to the act of accepting what has happened in the past while showing compassion and gentleness to yourself along the way. Forgiving yourself is about more than just putting the past behind you and moving on. It requires empathy, compassion, kindness, and understanding.

"The moment you know yourself you have known the most precious thing in existence."
-Osho

♡ **Love is mysterious**

Love is irrefutable and unpredictable. You can't decide when or how love will hit you. It can even come when you least expect it, and all you can do is to accept or deny it. With this mysterious nature, love also becomes magical, inspirational, and complex.

"Love encompasses so much, reaches so far, and heals so deeply, that any attempt to describe it, no matter how poetic, only dilutes it."
– **Steve Maraboli**

♡ **Love is ambiguous**

Love is simple, yet complicated. It is the source of happiness, but can also be the cause of the most intense pain that you can experience. Love is both the cure for misunderstandings and the cause of hostilities.

"Love cannot be explained, yet it explains all."
–**Elif Shafak**

♡ **Love is acceptance and commitment**

Love, in its purest form, is unconditional. It requires complete and total acceptance. When you welcome love with an open heart, you accept the totality of someone's personhood, including their flaws, broken pieces, and imperfections, while honoring the unparalleled beauty that's within them. Although it is an inherent capacity that you carry, love is also a choice of accepting and committing. Welcoming love is as critical as receiving it as you journey through life.

"We are all the best versions of ourselves when we have love and acceptance in our lives."
–**Dianna Agron**

♡ Love is a skill

Love, as a skill, recognizes that one size doesn't fit all. That you can be at different stages, that you have different experiences and perspectives. Like any other skill, it takes time and effort for it to be successful. When you look at love as a skill, it takes into account the imperfect nature of love and people. It challenges you to evaluate your love and relationships and to find the areas that you need to improve. Love is a skill that you should constantly try to cultivate.

Find the love you seek, by first finding the love within yourself. Learn to rest in that place within you that is your true home.
- **Sri Sri Ravi Shankar**

What Makes Love Beautiful?

Although imperfect, love is eternal and universal. It is immeasurable, and that's the beauty of it. Because when you remember the limitless nature of love within you, you become less self-serving and can selflessly share the gift of love.

Love creates a connection that makes you feel alive and allows you to realize your existence. It makes you feel that you have a purpose. and that you're not alone. It allows you to feel like you're finally home, safe and secured.

There are many reasons why love is considered as one of the most beautiful things in this world. Here are some of the few:

- ♡ Love gives hope
- ♡ Love makes the world beautiful
- ♡ Love makes you appreciate yourself, others, and life in general
- ♡ Love gives you a reason to live, improve, and grow
- ♡ Love is where your other emotions - joy, pain, laughter, bliss, excitement, anxiety, fear, courage, come from
- ♡ Love takes you closer to the true nature of your being

Anything flourishes with the nourishment of your compassion and appreciation. Love may stretch you and break you, but it can also put you back together as the most beautiful version of yourself. Love is what gives life meaning and purpose.

Do You Need Love to Survive?

Love is the essence of life; it takes on different forms and plays various roles in your everyday journey. **YES! You need love to survive,** for living life without love is next to mere existence. Love makes life worth living. It greatly influences how you interact with others and provides an inner compass on how you behave and direct your other emotions.

As social beings, we're all wired to engage in social interactions. Nurturing- an essential element of love is regarded as one of mankind's vital needs. The absence of love can cause loneliness and isolation, which also leads to a higher chance of having chronic health conditions and a decrease in overall health, especially for adults.

Love has been the ultimate key to the harmonious functioning of society for years. As a human being, you thrive on social interaction and relationships. You have this inherent need to experience strong bonds and connections. So, without love, you will have no drive to function as a person and as part of the larger community.

Take Action!

This next challenge is for you to open the door towards understanding love, promoting self-love, appreciation, gratitude, and willingness.

1. For the first day, recite some affirmations to start your day.

> I choose peace.
> I will succeed today.
> I am worthy of everything that I desire.
> My potential to succeed is limitless.
> It's okay to make mistakes; they don't define me and my whole story
> There is nothing that I can't do if I put my mind and effort into it

2. For the second day, disconnect from social media even for just a few hours (or a whole day if you can). Use your free time to discover more about yourself. You can also read books, travel, look for a new hobby, or aspire to learn a new skill.

3. For the third day, Move your body and exercise. This could be in any form of physical movement, from gentle stretching to high-energy dancing. What matters most is that you are enjoying yourself and that it makes you feel good inside out.

4. For the fourth day, write on a piece of paper everything you dislike about your situation at present, your limiting beliefs, and your negative judgment towards yourself. You can list down as many as you can, but be gentle with yourself while reflecting on everything that's been dragging you for some time now. After listing them, destroy the piece of paper by either ripping, burning, or covering it with paint. While doing this, reflect on the things you're letting go of. Whatever it is, take all the time you need to mourn what is no more, and willingly take in what's coming next, because it's going to be great, and beyond anything you can ever imagine.

To be asked: "What is love?" is perhaps the most complex and complicated question mankind has to answer. Love is a powerful energy that is ultimately universal and eternal that every person, from all walks of life, can understand. We all have our own interpretation of love that we had established from our personal stories and experiences. Being a limitless ability, love is also ever changing. It continuously grows and evolves. How we define it today may be different from how we view it tomorrow. But no matter how we view love, one thing's for certain. That love's ever-present and it resides in all of us.

The beauty of love is incomparable, it is ever-persistent, It never loses faith, it is always hopeful and enduring. It has a way of finding us when we least expect it. It motivates, inspires, and heals us. It transforms and brings out the best in us.

"Accept yourself, love yourself, and keep moving forward. If you want to fly, you have to give up what weighs you down."
- Roy T. Bennett

Chapter 5

Building & Cultivating Careers Through Relationships

"Coming together is a beginning. Keeping together is progress. Working together is success."
-Henry Ford

Healthy and successful relationships are essential to meaningful and fulfilling work life. In the world of vocation, all of us are interdependent on one another. We are governed by the linkages we build through our relationships, as these are the greatest assets that we can possess. With this in mind, we should make every effort to protect and invest in these invaluable connections.

Wherever you stand in the business relationship continuum, whether you're an employer or employee, stakeholder or partner, the relationships you build will become the foundations of your succeeding achievements. Your relationships may entail effort and hard work, but like anything important in life, they should be patiently built and preserved.

I've always believed that we don't meet people by accident. That every person we encounter has a role to play in our story. In the same way that we are playing an important part in their lives, and that our paths cross for a reason.

My professional journey began when I signed up for an internship while completing my undergrad at the University of Arizona. Selling books from one house to another wasn't as easy as I expected it to be. Lacking confidence and courage, I experienced a lot of rejections. But I used that as my motivation to try to do better. I challenged myself to adapt and be flexible. During the process, I met people who helped me realize my strengths and capitalize on them. I started my career from the bottom and climbed my way to where I am now. All of these I owe to the people who played their part, may it be big or small, in my success story.

My humble beginnings taught me that life is a meaningful tapestry of events that eventually leads you to your rightful place. It also showed me the value of respect. That we are all living our success story and we're just on a different timeline, but we'll all get there. So, treat everyone, regardless of stature in life, with the same compassion, love, and respect you aspire to receive. We are all worthy.

Through this journey, I want you to remember that you are the CEO of your life's calling. How far you go towards achieving the goals you aspire in your career, is in the palm of your hands. But the relationships you build along the way are essential and shouldn't be overlooked, for they empower you to confidently and courageously take risks, continually innovate, and recover from the setbacks you encounter. In this chapter, I invite you to take a closer look at the importance of connections in your career and reflect on the ways of building and cultivating healthy and lasting relationships.

> *"When we seek for connection, we restore the world to wholeness. Our seemingly separate lives become meaningful as we discover how truly necessary we are to each other."*
> –Margaret J. Wheatley

What Are Professional Relationships?

Work relationships are the linkages or connections that exist between all the units (stakeholders) in conducting business or in your career journey. This includes the employer/s, employees, managers, outsourced business partners, and all other personnel that your work position is associated with.

Creating and cultivating healthy relationships will not only make you more efficient, they'll also have a huge impact on your well-being by influencing your feelings of self-worth and belongingness. Healthy relationships cultivate trust, loyalty, and mutual respect, which are all beneficial for any line of profession.

What Are the Different Types of Relationships in The Workplace?

1. Employer-Employee Relationship

This relationship refers to the connection shared among the employees, either from the same or different teams. The employees should be comfortable with each other to make the relationship work, while the superiors or managers are given the task to make sure that the employees are working under favorable conditions and that conflicts are resolved and discouraged.

A healthy and strong relationship among the employees and the employers would benefit the whole company, for the working environment will be filled with mutual respect, happiness, productivity, trust, and loyalty. All of this will positively affect the company or business in the long run.

2. Relationship with the Customers

A customer is any person or institution that consumes, purchases, or receives a product or a service that a business is producing. The main goal of any business is to attract clients or customers and entice them to try, and in the long run, patronize their brand.

In building a healthy relationship with your customer, you'll be benefited in two ways: First, your customers will engage with your offers and buy your products or services, Second, they can refer your brand to other potential customers by providing great feedback and by telling their contacts reviews about the positive experience they've had with your brand.

By fostering relationships, you can transform your customers into your brand supporters, and they can become an integral part of our business growth and success.

3. Corporate Relationships

This refers to any sustainable relationship between a company and a nonprofit organization that provides value to both. These relationships are cause and mission-related. They are often initiated by the nonprofit organization, but can also be started from the corporate side. The main purpose of creating corporate relationships is to support the organization's mission.

4. Legal Relationships

Your legal relationships in business are valuable in achieving clarity in your mission. Although you don't need to work with your legal team regularly, it is important for you to establish healthy relationships with them, as they can ensure that the business is running in compliance with all the laws (local, state, or federal) and this can help you prevent future legal problems.

5. Relationship with Competitors

A competitor is a person, a team, business, or company who operates in the same industry, produces similar products or services, and targets the same customers that an entity also does. In business, we refer to competitors as rivals.

You can grow your business by the use of this relationship. Whenever your rivals are gaining higher market share, you can be more motivated to work harder, and when they are failing, it can be used as your insights about the things or actions you need to avoid. When it comes to innovation, seeing your competitors trying something new can raise the bar greatly and inspire you to innovate and think in advance.

A healthy competitive relationship with your competitors can give you the push you need to advance, expand, innovate, and be competent in your career.

So, What Defines a Good Work Relationship?

A healthy relationship in the workplace would require the values of mutual respect, trust, self-awareness, and open communication.

✓ **Respect** is considered the cornerstone of every relationship. It indicates acknowledging and validating the needs and feelings of all the individuals who are involved in the flow of your profession.

The presence of respect in the working environment will help you resolve conflicts faster and decrease your stress in the workplace. This would, in turn, increase your productivity, camaraderie, and sense of belonging.

✓ **Trust** is equated to transparency in the workplace. It indicates the comfortability in relying on and confiding to our team and is the feeling of safety and security that allows a harmonious interaction between a business and all its stakeholders.

Every business should work to earn the trust of the whole organization, and every interaction should be used as an opportunity to create healthy relationships that are nurtured with trust.

With this trust, your brand becomes believable. Customers and investors will have the best interest in mind. The business then operates with a culture of trustworthiness and affirms the organization with transparency and accountability.

✓ **Self-awareness** allows leaders to identify the flaws and gaps in managerial skills and reflect on the areas in which they are most effective. With this information, you can capitalize on your strengths and improve the areas that need polishing.

Having awareness and being accepting of your feelings will affect the performance of your career directly. It will open opportunities for improvement and transformation. It will also give you a clear sense of purpose and reaffirmation of both your uniqueness and your value as a team member.

✓ **Open Communication** in the business area is the process of sharing information between people from inside and outside a company. It is how the employees and the management interact to reach a certain goal. Business organizations aren't just faceless entities, they are made of real people and involve real-life situations. Therefore, the communication needed in your relationships would also be needed in interacting with your workgroup.

The Role of Communication in Work Relationships

Healthy relationships are considered the key to all your ventures in life, especially in this age of technology and advancement. Communication, may it be internal or external, needs to be clear for it to serve its purpose effectively. In this section, we will look into the different roles of communication in business relations.

♡ Information Exchange

Communication is valuable in the process of relaying information between people who make up the business organization. It can be with your employer, clients, suppliers, or employees. Open and healthy business communication allows a flawless exchange of ideas and updates. It results in productivity, effectiveness, and happiness for every team member.

♡ Goal Achievement

Being a key element of human behavior, communication in the workplace helps in aligning workers to work harmoniously and achieve the objectives of an organization. Good communication plays a vital role in almost every facet of any organization. Whether it be in management, product development, or customer relations.

The employees are considered the key audience in business communication, as they often serve as the channel of information to other audiences. If employees are informed and engaged, communications with other stakeholders will be strong and healthy as well.

♡ **Decision-making**

Effective communication helps the organization make better decisions and reach its goals. By communicating with all the team members, and taking in their ideas, points of view, and opinions, the organization can perform more efficiently and productively. Through effective communication, employees become more aware of what is happening internally, this increases the probability of cooperation and coordination and the decisions will be carried out more smoothly and successfully. Also, communication in the workplace helps in identifying existing problems and working towards solving them.

For Communication to Be Healthy And Open, It Needs To Be:

✓ Clear and Concise
✓ Complete and Concrete
✓ Courteous and Considerate
✓ Open and Accepting

"To effectively communicate, we must realize that we are all different in the way we perceive the world and use this understanding as a guide to our communication with others."
– Tony Robbins

How To Build & Nurture Professional Relationships

There are various ways to build professional relationships. These are habits, which when done authentically, consistently, and with utmost sincerity, will help you nurture and cultivate the professional relationships you desire.

1. **Care**- For you to cultivate and nurture relationships, both personal and professional, you have to care about people; their thoughts, emotions, feelings, and their well-being. As the saying by Theodore Roosevelt goes, "People don't care how much you know, until they know how much you care." Yes, your professional knowledge and expertise matter, of course, but caring for the people you're in a relationship with would shape how you go through your everyday living, and your success, in the long run.

2. **Listen**- This may appear to be so simple, yet it is often overlooked. The act of listening helps you understand others better. It also builds trust and makes others feel important. It is one of the key skills in professional development,

for listening helps you become more aware of your surroundings.

3. **Be reliable**- By being reliable, one can create deeper and more meaningful relationships. But to cultivate a healthy one, relationships should be built first on trust; For without this, the connections will wither and die.

4. **Offer and give help, without expecting something in return**- In building successful relationships, you should strive to establish yourself as both a listener and helper. Helping even in small ways will go a long way.

5. **Follow-up and stay in touch**- Your professional relationships won't grow, unless they are nurtured and cared for. They need time, effort, and genuine care.

The Importance of Professional Relationships

Building and cultivating professional relationships has a lot of benefits for both your personal and professional advancement, but one of the most important ones is to accelerate and advance your career. Having linkages and building relationships is fundamental to your long-term career. The other advantages include:

✓ **It creates an image for the company you belong to and yourself**

Image is considered the intangible connection between the company and all the people that comprise it. It is a powerful tool that is defined by emotions and connections. It can be compared to a relationship that exists between a couple, as it won't be made possible without the linkages that are founded on mutual trust, respect, and unity.

Businesses are initially faceless corporate entities and it is only by fostering healthy and positive relationships that we can create a unique face for our organization. One that is relatable and appealing.

✓ **It creates loyalty**

With loyalty being a lifelong investment for any venture, every person needs to cultivate and nurture the relationships they build, both internal and external. By building positive relationships with your team members, especially with your clients, you can transform your professional image into a brand that anyone can trust.

Creating loyalty through your relationships isn't something that happens overnight. It takes a lot of your commitment before they begin to materialize, and the results will be in congruence with the time you spent nurturing your relationships. The more you nurture it, the more successful your professional life becomes.

✓ **It breeds respect and builds a team that you can trust**

Every business strives to build the most competent and productive team. But to create the best team, good relationships should first be built within the company. By developing healthy and mutually respectful relationships, you'll be able to create an atmosphere that is conducive to the development of an alliance with a strong sense of camaraderie and teamwork.

By creating and nurturing good relationships in your professional career, you'll be able to increase job satisfaction, commitment, and productivity- the factors that define the best team.

"Every great business is built on friendship."
-James Cash Penney

Take Action!

This next challenge is for you to acknowledge the importance of relationships for your professional advancement, and a calling to work towards building and cultivating healthy relationships.

For the first day, reflect on the following questions:

1. Is group communication affecting your performance as a member of a team?

2. What are the difficulties you are experiencing in your professional life?

3. Is it important to know your teammates better? And are you willing to go the extra mile and know them genuinely?

4. How can you build healthy and lasting professional relationships in the workplace? What are the values you need to make this possible?

5. Identify your strengths and weaknesses as a team member. List down three (3) of your strong points and 3 things you'd like to work on yourself as a team member.

6. Before going to sleep, sit comfortably and close your eyes. Reflect on how your day went and what you want to accomplish in your line of work, and for the days to come. You can also journal your emotions and/or the lessons you've learned throughout the day, and what will be your concrete plan for you to have a purposeful tomorrow.

7. Be accountable and execute this challenge for a week. On the 8th day, reflect on the changes that the challenge has brought to your life.

"Teamwork sits alongside trust, communication, and tolerance as a building block of the best relationships. Teamwork is not "What can I get out of this relationship?" it's "What can I bring to this relationship to make it better?"

-Zero Dean

Chapter 6

Nurturing Your Inner Circle

"Family and friends are hidden treasures, seek them and enjoy their riches."
– Wanda Hope Carter

When it comes to life's meaning and happiness, the people closest to your heart matter the most. As a human being, you cannot thrive on your own. You need your family, friends, and everyone in your inner circle to serve as your pillars of support and motivation, especially when you are faced with life's hurdles and obstacles. With the help of your loved ones, you'll be able to live a life full of meaning and purpose. Indeed, they are life's greatest treasures, and being an invaluable part of your life, your task is to cherish and treasure the bonds you build with them.

Having the support and love of the people dearest to you does not only let you live a life full of happiness and love, but it also allows you to face every tomorrow with purpose and motivation. The broad networks that you build in life undoubtedly contribute to your growth, happiness, and feelings of achievement, but your inner circle- your family and friends, provide you greater meaning and support in life.

2020 and 2021 were years of growth and improvement for me. It was when I deepened my relationship with my partner, thrived with the company I was working with, a year when I launched two businesses, and when I learned the most about the value of my inner circle.

It was also a period of personal awakening. As I started letting go of what I had no control of and began loving the person I was becoming, countless blessings and opportunities opened for me- the greatest of which is the gift of motherhood.

I've always prayed for this day, when I'd carry the title of a "Mother". So, I had prepared myself and worked as hard as I could to be able to give my baby the best possible life that she deserves. Finding out I was pregnant ignited something inside me and inspired me to become the best version of myself.

From the moment I carried my Charlee into the world, I knew my life would change incredibly. I've never perceived the title "mother" as one of glamour nor pride. But when I held her for the first time, I could not think of a title I could cherish more. Everything felt surreal when I held my Charlee for the first time, and that's when it hit me. I was able to bring forth life. A beautiful, unparalleled, and sacred life.

My motherhood journey wouldn't be as blissful and as happy as it is now, without the help of my loved ones and my inner circle who showered me and my Charlee with their unending love, support, and guidance. It is during times like this that I thank my lucky stars for the wonder that is family.

As you move forward with me on this journey, I want you to acknowledge the value of your intimate relationships. To be grateful for every single day that you've been blessed to be with your loved ones and to strive to tighten your bonds and let your inner circle know that they are valued, cherished, and loved. As you strive to make a positive change in the world, start with your intimate relationships first. Make a conscious effort to mend the broken connections and strengthen the thriving ones.

When was the last time you made your family and your loved ones feel your care and appreciation? Whenever that may be, I want you to do it again today. With the uncertainties that we're all facing now, the most precious gift in our palm is the moments we have left.

So, make the most out of your limited time. Hold your family and friends, not in desperation, but in gratitude.

> *"There is no greater happiness for a man*
> *than approaching a door at the end of a day*
> *knowing someone on the other side of that door*
> *is waiting for the sound of his footsteps."*
> – Ronald Reagan

Your Intimate Relationships Are the Keys to Your Overall Health and Happiness

There are various reasons why your inner circle is the most important relationship that you should strive to build and cultivate. In this section, we'll take a closer look at some of these.

1. Your inner circle gives you a sense of security

One of the most important things that your inner circle provides is emotional security. Having a healthy foundation allows each member to develop a positive sense of self, which includes confidence, trust, and belief in oneself, in others, and the world. Emotional security is given by your intimate relationships and also gives you the courage and determination that you will need in facing any adversities in life.

2. Your inner circle gives you a sense of belonging

Having a strong sense of belonging and acceptance is vital for success and happiness in life. If you have a strong source of emotional support, nurturing, protection, warmth, and security, then, healthy human development becomes attainable. With your inner circle, you'll realize that wherever you may go in life, you'll always have a home that you can return to.

3. Your inner circle helps you develop healthy life-coping skills

Having a healthy inner group will help you learn and develop life skills that will allow you to make the best choices later in life. It will also serve as a firm foundation for your identity development, enabling you to feel comfortable and confident in trying new things and defying the limits you set for yourself.

4. Your inner circle gives you support and guidance

A strong and healthy support system is one where encouragement, love, support, and guidance are constantly given. It is also through the early interactions that you shape your characters and mold your principles in life. Through the guidance of the people around you, you'll be able to live a life of meaning and purpose.

Your Inner Relationships Matter

Relationships of any form are complex and important. The bonds that you form with other people throughout your life are vital to your overall well-being. But your innermost linkages are the foundations that will guide you on the succeeding connections you'll later build in life. Like food and water that nourish your physical body, your relationships sustain your mental and emotional wellness.

But with life's adversities and its dynamic nature, sometimes it becomes easy for you to let your borrowed time just pass by without acknowledging the really important thing. Without letting the people you hold close to your heart know how much you love them.

No. You are never promised tomorrow. So, this is a plea, a dare, and an invitation for you, not to miss out on the opportunity of making each member of your inner circle feel loved and valued today.

> *"The only rock I know that stays steady, the only*
> *institution I know that works, is the family."*
> **–Lee Iacocca**

So, How Can You Nurture Your Inner Circle?

The bonds that you build with your inner circle are made up of years of treasured memories- both joyous and sad, experiences that molded you to be the person that you are now, and interactions that you'll carry throughout your journey. Losing connections and drifting apart inevitably happens, but the positive part about your relationships is that you can do something to nurture and sustain them. In this section, we'll look into the various ways by which you can enhance your bonds with your loved ones.

♡ **Respect & value family time**

With your fast-paced life and conflicting schedules, making room for family time can be difficult. What you may fail to see and acknowledge is that there are many benefits to regularly connecting with your loved ones. No matter how busy your schedule is, you should be aware that your family needs you, the same way you need them. Spending time with your family and loved ones will help you mend broken bonds, feel reconnected, and have a strong foundation that you can lean on whenever you are faced with the uncertainties of life.

♡ **Appreciate & be grateful**

When it comes to strengthening your friendship and interpersonal relationships, gratitude is your best tool. After all, it is considered the most accessible and invaluable emotion that your inner circle needs. Gratitude provides a boost of positive emotion for both the receiver and the sender of the appreciation. Even just a simple act of saying "Thank you" can create feelings of esteem, trust, affection, and closeness.

♡ **Nurture each other's social & emotional needs**

In building strong and healthy bonds with your loved ones, you must let them feel that they are worthy, that they are loved and respected. Nurturing your bonds to be a place of security and safety is one of the main goals that you need to aim for as a group. With the daily stressors that you may face, it's vital to have a space where you can talk about your feelings and where you can get the support and guidance you need.

♡ Be accountable for your own shortcomings; forgive others & forgive yourself

Disagreements and misunderstandings are normal in any relationship. Everyone makes mistakes, but forgiveness and understanding are needed to move past these obstacles and foster a stronger relationship. You need to acknowledge your flaws and shortcomings, and through the process, become a better version of yourself. Loving comes with forgiving and acceptance both for yourself and others.

Being accountable for your mistakes is also vital for your growth as an individual and the flourishing of your relationships. Viewing accountability for your mistakes as an opportunity to learn will allow your inner circle to become a place that fosters healthy and holistic well-being. By being accountable and forgiving in your relationships, you can build a bond that is founded on trust, empowerment, and support.

♡ Be accepting

In fostering healthy and successful bonds, genuine acceptance is one of the keys needed. At times, you may overlook this fact because of the inevitable longing for perfection. Building bonds with your inner circle requires respect and acceptance of your loved ones' personhood- flaws and all. By accepting them genuinely, you'll be able to treat them as human beings who are capable and worthy of love and respect. So, give them the love that you also want to receive. Let them know that they matter and they are worthy.

♡ **Set healthy boundaries**

Your relationships can only thrive when the connections continue to grow positively. This makes setting healthy boundaries one of the most important keys in showing your love to your inner circle. Knowing that it's impossible to love someone without respect, setting healthy boundaries becomes crucial to the health of a relationship, for they are the proof and sign of respect.

In setting them, boundaries need to be clear, reasonable, and fair. They need to be consistent with the values you honor and the principles that you hold.

"Families are the compass that guides us. They are the inspiration to reach great heights, and our comfort when we occasionally falter."
–Brad Henry

Take Action!

This challenge is for you to reflect on your relationships and aspire to foster and nurture a healthier and purposeful inner circle.

1. Go to your chosen haven early in the morning or late in the afternoon. Take a moment to assess your social wellness by asking yourself the following questions:

   > Have you been feeling more connected with your loved ones recently?
   > Is there someone you can reach out to for support when you need it?
   > Which relationships do you value the most?
   > What kinds of interactions motivate you and what kinds drain you?
   > Why are communities important to you?
   > How can you be more connected to your family? Friends? Or to your social group?

2. Pause for a moment and think of the people whom you feel grateful for. In your journal, write a special note of about 2-3 sentences to each one of them.

3. Allot an hour of "present-time" where you put your devices and other distractions away and focus on being present and engaging in meaningful conversation or shared experience.

4. Before going to sleep, sit comfortably and close your eyes. Reflect on how your daily interaction with your loved ones went and think of what you want to accomplish socially for the day to

come, you can also journal your emotions about what you've learned throughout the day, and what will be your concrete plan for you to have a purposeful tomorrow.

5. Execute this challenge for a week. On the 8th day, reflect on the changes that the challenge has brought to your life. Continue the challenge until it becomes a habit.

Your physical and mental well-being are bounded by the quality of your personal relationships. The closer you are connected to the people you love, the happier you feel and the more satisfaction you'll have in your life. I want you to realize that these moments of connection with your loved ones are one of your most important life experiences. The relationships that you should strive to foster and cultivate do not only include that with your family and friends but also with the wider communities that you belong to. Forming healthy and thriving relationships make up your identity and allow you to live a purposeful life.

> *"Alone, we can do so little; together, we can do so much"*
> **- Helen Keller**

Lynee Palacios

Chapter 7

Cultivating Healthy Romantic Relationships

"Love is the beginning of the journey, its end, and the journey itself."
-Deepak Chopra

Look around, you are living in a dynamic and highly complex society that affects how you view the world and interact with those around you. In these uncertain times, who doesn't want to be loved? To be accepted for who one truly is? To be protected, to feel cared for and cherished? As a social being, you have been in pursuit of the love and acceptance that you deserve. It is in your nature, as human beings, to share your life and bond with others.

Your romantic relationships play an important role in fulfilling your innate needs for social connections, sexual relations, and intimacy. Romantic relationships, just like any other connections, thrive or wither, depending on how you cultivate them. And no matter how strong the foundation, your romantic relationship, without nourishment, cannot survive on its own. A healthy relationship requires time, attention, love, and willingness.

Regardless of how my past relationships turned out, I always remind myself that no love is ever wasted, none of them was a failure. Whether it ended or prospered, each one of them became part of the map I used to find myself, which eventually led me to the person I was destined to be with and the person I was supposed to become.

Looking back, I can say that all of them taught me valuable lessons on self-love, self-acceptance, and self-improvement. That we thrive on relationships as it is a human need. And to build positive relationships, we should first learn to be okay with ourselves and not depend on others to make us feel worthy. For it is only when we recognize our flaws and be vulnerable with our loved ones, can we grow and let the process of healing happen.

Meeting my partner and soon-to-be husband, Jerome, made me understand that love really comes in God's perfect time and with the compassion, respect, trust, and acceptance we have for each other, our love grows stronger each day.

Wherever your romantic relationship falls in the continuum of healthy connections, I want you to take the necessary steps to improve it. Make an effort to work on your relationship, and you will be rewarded with a deeper connection that will provide you the inspiration and direction you need to live a meaningful life.

In this little journey, I invite you to look at your romantic relationship as a tactical mission that requires foresight, strategy, and effort for it to thrive. I want you to nurture your relationship and aspire to build a healthier and stronger human connection.

"Being deeply loved by someone gives you strength while loving someone deeply, gives you courage."
-Lao Tzu

Love Makes the World Go Round

A nurturing, loving, and fulfilling relationship is one of the keys to living a meaningful life. It elicits positive feelings of happiness and contentment, but more importantly, it supports, inspires, and motivates individuals to achieve holistic wellness.

Your romantic relationship is one of the more important aspects of life. However, you may not fully understand what is needed in creating a healthy and ideal relationship. So, in this section, we'll look into the keys to a better loving relationship that allows a new level of passion, romance, and intimacy. By understanding these keys, you'll be able to develop the tools and techniques that will allow you to build and cultivate healthy romantic relationships.

Essential Traits in Building & Cultivating Healthy Romantic Relationships:

Healthy and Effective Communication is the act of communicating that is considered the foundation that becomes the basis for which other traits are built. It is vital for a long and fulfilling relationship and involves a balance of the two communication mediums- talking and listening.

In your romantic relationships (or in any relationship you build), you should strive to balance the act of talking and listening. When your partner is communicating with you, be sure to listen without judgment, but with an open mind. Avoid interrupting and be attentive to the words and the tone of voice of your partner. The facial expressions and gestures of your partner can also give you insight into what they're trying to impart. By being observant, you can find some hints as to how they're really feeling, their beliefs, and their perspectives. It will also give you a vivid understanding of what the relationship needs for it to be meaningful and satisfying for you and your partner.

Before communicating your thoughts, strive to gain a fuller picture of the situation. Delay your responses with necessary pauses, after your partner finishes speaking. Then, identify what your partner is indirectly or directly highlighting. After that, summarize what you understood, confirm this with your partner, and with empathy, communicate what you think of the situation or the topic. While doing this, be mindful of not talking over or misunderstanding your partner's point.

If you experience most of the signs stated below, it means you need to work on your relationship's communication:

- ✓ Using aggressive speech such as raising your voice, blaming or criticizing, controlling or dominating the conversation
- ✓ Using passive-aggressive behavior in communicating: cracking jokes about your partner's mistakes, punishing by giving the silent treatment, insulting or sarcastically mocking them about their decisions
- ✓ Simply avoiding or ignoring conflicts or issues

You can communicate more effectively by:

♡ **Being cautious and conscious of your partner's feelings**- Most often, couples begin a conversation by nagging or placing blame on the other. To counter this, use less accusatory language and begin your statements by expressing how you feel. For example, instead of calling out your partner for not spending more time with you, you can say "I feel hurt when you spend more time with your friends," which is less accusatory compared to the statement, "You are always with your friends."

♡ **Setting your boundaries**- By placing clear and firm boundaries, you can avoid the effects of miscommunication. For example, when it comes to your expenses, come up with a clear plan or boundary on your budget for the week. By doing this, you can avoid future issues on financial matters.

♡ **Avoid silent treatment**- Boundary-setting works best when it is communicated explicitly with a partner. Most partners give the silent treatment in communicating their need for boundaries. By not properly conveying your needs, preferences, and boundaries, your partner may not realize when they've crossed one.

♡ **Avoid bringing up the past**- A healthy relationship strives for unconditional positive regard. This is when you support your partner to grow and better themselves. It also involves making every effort to keep the peace and understanding in the relationship. Moving past old mistakes together is one of the keys to a healthy and genuine relationship.

♡ **Avoid yelling or screaming**- Resorting to yelling or screaming during an argument is one of the most ineffective ways of communicating your feelings of frustration or anger, your needs, or opinions. Raising your voice during an argument doesn't resolve any issue and most of the time only intensifies the situation. It also leads to deteriorating your partner's self-esteem. So, if you are in the middle of an argument and your partner starts to raise a voice, don't yell back in retribution. Instead, communicate clearly that you're willing to talk respectfully but aren't participating if your partner is going to yell. Be willing to end the conversation if necessary and make sure to sort things out if both parties have already cooled down and are willing to sort things out respectfully.

"Communication to a relationship is like oxygen to life. Without it... it dies."
-Tony Gaskins

Respect. Understanding and valuing your partner's opinions and your differences are fundamental in building and nurturing healthy relationships. Disagreements are inevitable, but respecting the differences in perspective and beliefs allows one to foster compassion and breeds a deeper sense of connection. It's natural and valid to disagree, but you should do this with respect and acceptance.

Below are the signs that respect in the relationship is lacking and shouldn't be overlooked.

- ✓ Partner's boundaries are ignored- Healthy relationships are built on established boundaries that are acknowledged and respected. So, if a partner repeatedly ignores or completely disregards yours, it's clearly a sign of a lack of respect. Crossing the boundary can take many forms, and often gets worse over time and none of it should be taken lightly.

- ✓ Using insecurities against a partner- A good relationship is where you feel safe enough to open up, share deep thoughts, and lean on for comfort, understanding, and support.

- ✓ Not valuing partner's time- Constantly changing your plans just because your partner doesn't approve or has other plans, or putting your dreams on hold to accommodate your partner's needs, or when they show a lack of regard and interest in what you value is a clear sign of disrespect which is inappropriate.

✓ Display of self-centered attitude- when you and your partner think of yourselves before the other, you'll have trouble arguing in a civil way. You may tend to dig in their heels to insist they're right. Being self-absorbed and needing your constant approval, accolades, and attention, but rarely returning those gifts to you.

You can foster a respectful romantic relationship by:

♡ Seeing your partner as a person worthy of respect
♡ Accept, appreciate and love your partner for who they are
♡ Communicate your thoughts to your partner
♡ Treat your partner as someone who's inherently valuable

"Respect is one of the greatest expressions of love."
– Don Miguel Ruiz

Honesty. Honesty comes from genuine and open communication. It means always being truthful and open, for both small and big things. It indicates being true to oneself and avoiding pretensions, whether it be on your words, thoughts, or actions.

Honesty is also considered the foundation for trust- which is necessary for a relationship to thrive and function. Being trustworthy and honest helps you and your partner to hold promises and commitments.

The signs listed below will tell you that your relationship lacks honesty:

   ✓ Using indirect or nonspecific speech- a dishonest relationship is emotionally draining, for instead of providing reasonable facts, lying is used as the easiest choice. A dishonest partner cannot be held accountable because it's easier for them to lie now than to talk about problems.

   ✓ Being too defensive- when one becomes overly defensive over the simplest of things, it shows anticipation or perception of threat in their environment, which becomes a huge problem for any relationship.

   ✓ Emotional disconnection- This occurs when one feels disconnected, lonely, or detached from the relationship instead of feeling the closeness they admired earlier in their relationship.

"The establishment of any relationship, both individual and expert, is honesty."
– Alexander Mejia

Trust. Honesty in a relationship allows trust to come naturally. It entails believing in yourself and others, whether it be in their judgments, plans, or motives.

Without trust, a relationship will become dysfunctional and chaotic. Having trust in your romantic partnership brings in a sense of peace and tranquility.

Failure in building trust in the relationship will make you feel insecure and unsafe. It will eventually lead to even more complications in the relationship that may at times cause its failure.

If you experience most of the signs below, it means you need to work on your relationship's level of trust:

- ✓ Being overprotective out of fear that your partner will be disloyal
- ✓ Finding it hard to forgive the smallest mistakes
- ✓ Feeling like you can't let your guard down in front of your partner
- ✓ Being excessively and unreasonably wary of other people's presence in your relationship
- ✓ Wanting to distance yourself and your partner from other people
- ✓ Refusing to be committed to a relationship
- ✓ Assuming and awaiting betrayal
- ✓ Secretly watching their social media activity

How to foster an honest and truthful relationship

- ♡ Be consistent.
- ♡ Don't commit to things you can't do.
- ♡ Be truthful with your reactions
- ♡ Admit and own your mistakes
- ♡ Be sincere with your actions

"Trust leads to approachability and open communications."
– Scott Weiss

Other Essential Traits for A Healthy Romantic Relationship

For a romantic relationship to be healthy and successful, aside from the core traits, there are other essential traits that you should also cultivate in your relationship. This includes passion, intimacy, fun, adventure, and care. All of these traits provide excitement, joy, and spice to your relationship. Now, your goal is to cultivate every one of these supportive traits, and allow your relationship to be more satisfying, purposeful, and meaningful.

In your quest for a healthier and more meaningful romantic relationship, having shared goals, values, beliefs, and ideals, that are also in sync with your own goals as individuals will be the main keys.

Take Action!

This next challenge is aimed at allowing you to build and cultivate a healthier and purposeful romantic relationship.

1. Close your eyes and reflect on your romantic relationship. Describe its status by listing five to ten adjectives that would describe it.

2. In your journal, take some time to define the beginning, middle and present-day state of your relationship. For each time-stamp, I want you to note down how you felt during the different stages.

3. Take a moment and answer the following questions:

   What did you learn from your past relationship/s that you wish to carry into your present or next one?

   What are the things you think you need to work on yourself to have a more meaningful present or future romantic relationship?

4. Now, focus on your present romantic relationship. List down all the things that you need to change or improve to foster and cultivate a more meaningful and healthier relationship.

5. For the next task, create a vision card of what your aspired relationship looks like. Strive to be realistic and hopeful while doing this. For your vision card, glue a collection of images and word cut-outs that represent the relationship you desire to attract into your life.

6. Execute this challenge for a week. On the 8th day, reflect on the changes that the challenge has brought to your life.

"A healthy relationship is one in which love enriches you; not imprisons you."
- Steve Maraboli

Chapter 8

The Role of Communication in Healthy Relationships

"Communication is the lifeline of any relationship. Without it, the relationship will starve itself to death."
- Elizabeth Bourgeret

As we navigate our lives, we find ourselves in a constant search for a healthy connection that entails a feeling of alignment, compatibility, understanding, and belongingness between and among the people we come in contact with. This connection goes beyond physical or superficial attraction, mere conversations, or intellectual similarities. Instead, it connects us on a deeper level, where we feel a secure link that allows us to journey life with an unshakeable foundation.

In our constant and unwavering pursuit for this connection, we come to realize that the key to every human connection is healthy and effective communication. This also becomes the basis of our every interpersonal relationship. Without a doubt, communication plays a vital role in building our linkages, bridging the gap between human beings, and understanding one another.

Throughout my journey, I can say that my relationship with my inner circle has been healthy and thriving. But there came a time when I felt like something was missing in my life and that was having a meaningful and sincere romantic relationship. Having been in twelve relationships, none of which lasted longer than a year, I started questioning why it always doesn't seem to work out. Although it didn't feel like this at that time, I now consider breakups as healthy experiences that taught me something about myself and life in general and allowed me to cultivate healthier ways of relating.

In the past, I was always looking for a picture-perfect love story. But I was afraid to be vulnerable and let someone see the hidden parts of me. I felt it unnecessary to share the hardships I went through and open up when I was struggling.

Contemplating my past experiences, I realized that my difficulty of forming a healthy emotional bond with my significant other stems from the lack of healthy communication. I decided to change by striving to be more open and accepting. I also took a communication course that helped not only my career but also my personal journey. This was when I felt the change that I've been longing for in my life. Fresh from a breakup, I met my current partner, who came into my life unexpectedly but gave answers to all my why's.

Acknowledging my flaws and faults, and breaking patterns from my previous relationships was never an easy feat. But having Jerome in my life, I realized that there's a reason for everything and that as long as we're both willing to grow together, our relationship will also flourish.

If it weren't for our willingness to cultivate healthy communication and our unrelenting effort to be fully present, open, and honest, we wouldn't be in the relationship that we are in now, one that's rooted in unconditional love, trust, acceptance, and mutual respect.

Think for a moment and ask yourself: Do you have healthy connections with your social linkages? Are you communicating effectively? And, how can you build healthier and lasting relationships through communication?

For your next step in this journey, I invite you to reflect and check on your connections and aspire to build and cultivate healthier and more effective communication that will be the key to establishing your ideal relationships.

Allow me to help you open new doors leading you to a meaningful and more connected life. Your goal now is to begin to understand the value of healthy and effective communication in your life and discover what you can do to be a better communicator. Undoubtedly, communication is the key to a sound, loving, and trusting relationship.

"The most important thing in communication is hearing what isn't being said. The art of reading between the lines is a lifelong quest of the wise."
- Shannon L. Adler

What Is Communication?

Communication has various definitions, some of them include:

- ✓ The act or process of using sounds, signs, or behaviors to express or exchange information or to express your ideas, thoughts, and feelings to someone else.
  -Merriam Webster Dictionary

✓ The exchange of thoughts, messages, or information, as by speech, signals, writing, or behavior
- The Free Dictionary

✓ The imparting or exchanging of information by speaking, writing, or using some other medium
- Oxford Dictionary

Looking at the different definitions of communication, we can say that it is not limited to mere words, it also includes:

♡ The manner of expressing or communicating your thoughts- including the tone of voice and the time you communicate
♡ The intention or the message behind communicating
♡ What you don't say/ what you are indirectly saying
♡ Your body language and gestures
♡ Your facial expressions
♡ The media you use and its effectiveness in communicating

So, What Makes Communication Effective?

Effective communication is a skill that doesn't happen in an instant. It has to be constantly learned, cultivated, and improved. Effective communication is one where:

1. **The value of empathy is not disregarded**

   Empathy, in its simplest form, involves seeing things from the perspective of others. It is "putting yourself in another's shoe" to understand where the person is coming from or what the other person feels. In communication, empathy is regarded as one of the most important skills needed. It removes all the biases that you have, allowing you to avoid judgments and invalid conclusions that will lead to miscommunication.

2. **Listening goes beyond hearing, it also needs comprehension and attentiveness**

   Listening in the communication process is fundamental and to do this effectively, you have to give your full attention when someone is trying to convey their idea or opinion. The act of listening effectively will go a long way in building a lasting and healthier relationship.

3. **Non-verbal communication is given emphasis**

   Body language and gestures greatly impact the flow of communication in your relationship. It is also essential in showing one's empathy while conversing. Maintaining eye contact, using appropriate tone of voice and hand gestures, as well as smiling when the situation calls for it, all of these create a difference in the communication process.

4. Questions are asked to further understand the information being conveyed

Effective communication is a skill that has to be constantly learned, cultivated, and improved. In improving your communication skills, you'll need to ask questions while conversing. This will show that you are interested in the discussion and allow the people you're talking with to feel more comfortable and at ease to communicate their thoughts and opinions.

This also includes reflecting on the information shared and summarizing it to the party from whom the information was taken to avoid miscommunication and misinterpretation.

5. Active listening is harnessed

Effective communication includes both speaking and listening. By actively listening and responding to another person, you'll be able to understand messages better and realize that the best way to avoid the blocks in communication is by talking and listening actively, asking questions to clarify without interrupting, and respecting the points of the person you're talking with.

6. You strive to avoid any source of miscommunication

Miscommunication is failing to communicate ideas, thoughts, or intentions successfully. The various sources of miscommunication can be referred to as the barriers to effective and healthy communication.

Communication barriers block the meaning of the messages sent and conveyed. These blocks cause misunderstanding and confusion. The following are the different conversational blocks that may be present in your relationships:

♡ **Physical/ Emotional Barriers**

Your physical and emotional state greatly affects the effectiveness of communication. Whenever you feel anxious, sad, tired, sleepy, exhausted, or any other emotions that might impede how you convey your thoughts or opinions, it is best to be very cautious and know if it is the right time to speak or if the words that you'll be using are not based solely on what you feel. Do not allow your emotions to get the best out of you, as you might regret it afterward.

Having a poor emotional and physical state also inhibits you to pay close attention, listen well, understand, and react appropriately. This also includes your psychological interference. This is when an individual is under too much emotion, which affects the tone and overpowers the message you're trying to convey. This then becomes an obstacle in the communication process and leads to an emotional barrier.

To counter this, it is very important to be in your most comfortable state while conversing with other people. When you're in a heightened emotional state, you need to let your significant other know and try to discuss it later. Strive to be fully present and actively listen. For your romantic relationships, It is also very important that you both decide or set a specific time to discuss your day and talk about how your day went. It is best to do this before going to bed because it increases connection and intimacy.

Setting some ground rules for your everyday communication is helpful in avoiding miscommunication. Rules can include resolving issues before going to sleep, avoiding using electronic gadgets or any other distractions that may be a barrier to effective communication, or always letting the other finish their piece and waiting for your turn before speaking.

♡ Interruptions/Distractions

The communication process can be greatly affected by the present environmental and natural conditions while the sender is sending a message to the receiver. Noise, distance, connection, and other distractions are the most prominent barriers to communication. Fortunately, they are also the easiest barriers to be resolved.

Strive to be fully present and actively listen. The use of social media and television are considered as some of the major distractions in communication. One would lose interest in communicating if the other person is scrolling down their social media accounts. So, the first thing you need to do is to eliminate these barriers and any distractions while you converse. Be sure each party is actively listening and is given the chance to share their feelings.

♡ Non-verbal Cues

It is important to be aware that your non-verbal cues are as important as your verbal ones in communication. What you are conveying through words has to match what your actions and intentions are. It is very important to avoid sending mixed messages and bear in mind that body language can reinforce your spoken message or it can contradict it completely. Because of this, you should pay attention to your actions as well as your words when speaking with your significant others.

♡ Misconception

While conversing, it is sometimes unavoidable for one to misperceive what the other is saying. An example is when you think your partner is upset over one thing due to the tone of voice or the wrong choice of words, but they're upset about something else. These misunderstandings often lead to false feedback and can further lead to bigger problems.

The messages we're conveying may not be received exactly the way it was intended during the process. Hence, the communicator needs to seek feedback to check if their message was clearly understood. As a receiver, if you ever feel that you've perceived a piece of information wrongly, simply ask the person to clarify.

♡ Lack Of Concentration/ Focus

Low focus or lack of concentration is detrimental to effective communication. When your mind is preoccupied with other things while communicating, you'll not be able to form proper messages, listen to what others are saying, interpret the message, or give proper feedback. The communication process then becomes ineffective.

So, in communicating with others, if ever you feel that you lack concentration and focus, let the other person know that you are not in the right disposition to concentrate. Because when people feel like they're not being listened to, it may fuel anger and resentment.

"To effectively communicate, we must realize that we are all different in the way we perceive the world and use this understanding as a guide to our communication with others."
- Anthony Robbins

Take Action!

This challenge will help you understand the value of communication in building healthy and lasting relationships. It will also provide a venue for improving your communication skills that will allow you to strengthen your social connections.

1. Being attuned with your own emotions will be your foundation in building a healthier relationship through communication. Go to your chosen sanctuary and reflect on the way you communicate your feelings and thoughts to your loved ones. Do you think you're communicating effectively with your inner circle?

2. In your journal, identify your strengths and weaknesses in communication. List down Three of your strong points and 3 things you'd like to work on yourself when it comes to communicating with others. Congratulate yourself on your positive points. For your weak points, think of ways on how you can improve them. List two to three ways for each.

3. Before going to sleep, Sit comfortably and close your eyes. Reflect on how your day went and note how you communicate throughout the day. Were you able to convey your thoughts and listen to the opinions of others? Were you a good listener and a good sender of messages? You can also journal your emotions and/or the lessons about communication that you've learned throughout the day, and what will be your concrete plan for you to have a purposeful connection tomorrow.

4. Be accountable and execute this challenge for a week. On the 8th day, reflect on the changes that the challenge has brought to your life. Continue the challenge until it becomes a habit.

Effective communication goes beyond the exchange or relay of information. It becomes paramount to growth and is vital in fostering and culminating healthy and long-lasting relationships.

As social beings, we communicate to survive. It's about understanding the emotion and intentions and striving to have a clear, courteous, concise, concrete, complete, and coherent flow of information transmission.

"Communication is a skill that you can learn. It's like riding a bicycle or typing. If you're willing to work at it, you can rapidly improve the quality of every part of your life."
— **Brian Tracy**

Chapter 9

Strengthening Human Connections

"We all are so deeply interconnected; we have no option but to love all. Be kind and do good for anyone and that will be reflected. The ripples of the kind heart are the highest blessings of the Universe."
- Amit Ray

As you open your eyes to a new day, with a great ambition unfolding in your heart, a number of goals embedded in your mind, and an immense desire to make your mark on the world; you'll find that at the center of all these aspirations, lies an important thing that defies your existence- your innate drive as a human being, to feel connected.

Human connection is the exchange of positive energy between and among people. It is vital in your pursuit of a meaningful and happy life. It entails the feeling of belongingness, understanding, unity, trust, and love, among others. Through human connection, you'll feel the rewarding elements in life.

One of the most important lessons life has taught me is the value of the connections I build throughout my existence. Looking back as an unsure and timid girl, I can say that I've come a long way and I'm grateful for the communities that I'm a part of and those that I will still have the honor to be involved in. Being part of an inner circle is essential, but knowing that I'm part of an even bigger community motivates me even more to be a better version of myself, constantly inspire others, and create change.

From my experiences with my Mastermind Family to my Wonder Women Tribe, my VIAA Family, and my Intuitive Moms Community; I found the home that I've been searching for my whole life. Throughout my journey, I consider myself lucky to hear stories of people discovering their passion and following their dreams. I'll forever be proud to be part of these communities that are constantly creating opportunities and transforming countless lives.

"We are each other's harvest; we are each other's business; we are each other's magnitude and bond." Looking at the words of one of the most celebrated poets, and a Pulitzer Prize winner, Gwendolyn Brooks, and countless Sociological studies available to us, it is undeniable that we, as human beings, are innately social and are deeply molded by our linkages.

Through this journey, I want to inspire you to see the beauty of human connections, to be more socially connected, and understand the unerring role of your social nature in your happiness and success in life. It is in these uncertain times, that you'll need the support and love of these connections. The beauty of cultivating healthy human connections is that it provides a safe space for you to be courageous while allowing you to be vulnerable as well, one where you can share your thoughts and opinions and not be judged while enhancing the force that binds humans together. This chapter is for you to tighten loose connections and strive to be part of a healthy and purposeful community.

"Even the weak become strong when they are united."
- Friedrich von Schiller

So, What Is a Purposeful Community?

In its simplest form, a community is a collection of people occupying a certain place or having a particular characteristic in common. In other words, it is a social unit sharing the same characteristics such as identity, customs, values, religions, and locations. But a community shouldn't just be defined as a place or an idea. It's actually much bigger than that. For a community to be purposeful, you should attach the human relationship that it represents. A community is an assembly of people who care about each other and a place where the sense of belongingness is consistently validated and sustained.

> *"A healthy social life is found only, when in the mirror of each soul the whole community finds its reflection, and when in the whole community the virtue of each one is living."*
> **-Rudolf Steiner**

At the core of a community, commitment is the condition or state of being dedicated or devoted to a cause, activity, or relationship. It encompasses values such as trust, love, and devotion even when things get tough. It is one of the major pillars of a group or an organization and serves as a foundation and gives the group the strength it needs.

Being part of a community is very important because it serves as your anchor when faced with the tides of uncertainties. It gives you a sense of belonging, which is a human necessity, just like your need for food and shelter. Knowing that you belong is vital in realizing your lives' value and coping with intense emotions.

A community also helps shape your identity. Beyond simply being a physical place, it is what happens in the community; the experiences that the members share, both negative or positive, that start shaping your shared and unique forms of identity. It is in your community where you first find out who you are and what your purpose in life is. Furthermore, the community serves as your motivation and inspiration. Whether it be a small or vast community that you belong to, it is undeniable that by sharing the same mindset and priorities with your community members, you can work more inspired and motivated. Allowing you to evaluate your performance effectively and uplift each other. It fosters a sense of communal ownership and collective responsibility, from which success emerges.

"One of the marvelous things about community is that it enables us to welcome and help people in a way we couldn't as individuals."
– Jean Vanier

The Journey Towards Purposeful Human Connection

Most people think that yearning for a connection or support is a sign of weakness and dependence, what they may fail to realize is that it is actually a sign of strength. Because it is only in knowing yourself well enough, will you understand that you need others in your story and it is only in having the courage to share your personhood and be vulnerable, can you have this transforming experience. By sharing, you connect, and by connecting, you begin to heal. To start with your journey and foster healthy relationships, you will need to:

♡ Open your heart to the people around you and understand that they have love and hope inside them, just like you. Open your heart. Believe in yourself, and know that you are worthy of others' love as well. Let others in.

♡ Be thankful for your support group. Your family, friends, teammates, or even the people you haven't met yet served as your source of inspiration throughout your journey.

♡ Appreciate and make others feel special. Let the people you hold dear to your heart feel that you love and care for them. Give them the same amount of appreciation and understanding you'd like to receive.

♡ Smile, and be curious. If given a chance to build healthy relationships, I want you to see it as an opportunity, and seize it with all your heart. Cultivate an atmosphere that is cordial and relaxed. Smile, and appreciate what the people around you are sharing and strive to be a good listener. That simple smile will go a long way.

♡ Find clarity by diving into deeper conversations. Having one-on-one conversations, or even small group talks, and conversing about each other's struggles and challenges, aspirations, and life purposes, will make you feel more connected and relaxed.

"We cannot live only for ourselves. A thousand fibers connect us with our fellow men."
— Herman Melville

Take Action!

This challenge is for you to reflect on your relationships and aspire to build and cultivate a healthier and purposeful community.

1. For your first task on this challenge, as you sit comfortably on your chosen sanctuary, I want you to create some positive wishes or a mantra, which will be centered on giving good wishes to yourself and others.

   An example: "I declare that today will be a day full of positivity, contentment, good health, and love for me and my loved ones."

   As you repeat the mantra, picture your good wishes physically going from you to your loved ones.

2. For your second task, I want you to reflect on your social health and list three adjectives that can describe it.

3. Reflect on your social well-being by answering the following questions:

   Do you have people whom you think you can rely on?

Does any barrier inhibit your ability to have meaningful interactions with your community?
Do you think you are socially healthy and happy?
Do you constantly feel that you belong in your community?
What can you do to address the difficulties you are facing with your social life?

4. For the next task, create a vision card of what your aspired relationship looks like. Strive to be realistic and hopeful while doing this. For your vision card, glue a collection of images and word cut-outs that represent the relationship you desire to attract into your life.

5. Before going to sleep, sit comfortably and close your eyes. Reflect on how your daily interaction with your loved ones went and think of what you want to accomplish socially for the day to come, you can also journal your emotions about what you've learned throughout the day, and what will be your concrete plan for you to have a purposeful tomorrow.

6. Execute this challenge for a week. On the 8th day, reflect on the changes that the challenge has brought to your life. Continue the challenge until it becomes a habit.

As social beings, building healthy connections is essential to a meaningful and purposeful life. The bonds that you foster throughout your life affect your overall well-being. Without a doubt, it is one of the most powerful forces that either bind or divide the world. So, be a medium of connection and unity. Reach out to others and believe in the difference that you can make!

"Reach out and help others. If you have the power to make someone happy, do it. Be a vessel, be the change, be the difference, or be the inspiration. Shine your light as an example. The world needs more of that."
-Germany Kent

Lynee Palacios

Chapter 10

Be Inspired & Be an Inspiration

"We all serve as a vessel to be messengers for one another. Are you sharing the messages you are inspired to speak? Someone is waiting to hear your words."
- Nanette Mathews

For most of us, the previous years have been rough, tiring, and painful. Some may be carrying a heavier toll, but all carry a piece of baggage or two. Despite the load that each of us is carrying. It's really not the weight that matters, but the way we choose to carry it. So, carry on and believe in your potential. You may not be aware of this, but you have the power to be inspired and be an inspiration.

Living in a world with billions of others may make you feel insignificant, but what if I tell you that you have the power to change the world? To create something magnificent and contribute to the greatness of life? Every morning you wake up is an opportunity to make a difference. Everywhere you set your foot, you can be a source of inspiration and change others' lives forever through your little ways. For, changing the world isn't just about a single, grandiose act, it's through the unglamorous, little things you do every day that you're able to contribute and make a difference.

As a young girl longing to carve my own name and make my own mark, I was inspired by individuals who were sure of where they're going, who strived enthusiastically to reach their goals, and committed to accomplish what they set out to do and complete it with vigor and hope. I aspired to be like them, to get to where they have gotten, and follow in their footsteps.

The lessons I received from my mentors, inner circle and the people who I looked up to for years, paved the way for me and inspired me to dream and act and do whatever it takes to chase my goals. I yearn for my time to inspire others to transform their lives and through this book and the communities I founded, I want to be an instrument of change.

Through this journey, I hope you find the courage and determination to be more inspired and serve as an inspiration for others during the process. You hold great potential behind your doubts. If you only know the possibilities that you carry within yourself, you'll see the greatness that you are. It's time to reclaim your worthiness.

We are all inspired and motivated by the different things around us. But whatever the form may be, inspiration happens when the inner flame flares up and you feel the passion and motivation to be or to do something. Now, as you go through this adventure with me, I want you to feel more inspired and strive to inspire others as well and you can start by sharing your own life story. Your adventure.

Your story has the immense power to encourage and motivate others to overcome their obstacles. Your experiences can create a difference in the lives of others. For the pages ahead, I will provide you a venue for you to share your story. Start now and discover that the world is your stage, waiting for you to share your greatness with the rest of the world. Good luck!

"Every person on this planet has a story to tell, something that makes them unique adding to the whole."
- Madisyn Taylor

Why Are Stories Important?

Sharing stories is one of the most important means of influencing, teaching, and inspiring others. The impact of sharing one's story is undeniable and there are various reasons why.

♡ **Sharing stories forms a deeper sense of connection**

One of the strongest ways we can connect as social beings is through sharing stories. It allows us to understand and relate with each other and through this, form meaningful bonds. Sharing stories sparks an indispensable connection that holds the possibility of making a difference in someone's life. So, share your story every chance you get. For, these stories give others the chance to feel less lonely and more worthy.

♡ **Sharing your stories is both therapeutic and liberating**

Sharing stories and voicing out your experiences can be liberating. Whether it's shared with a public audience, a confidant, or for yourself, your spoken experiences have the power to heal. The more you illuminate your hidden narratives, the more you free yourself.

♡ **Sharing stories allows you to find your voice**

Learning to express yourself and reflect on your experiences are some of the few benefits that you can get from sharing your story. Effectively narrating your experiences and using them as a medium to influence and inspire others will make you realize that your voice matters, that your narratives matter.

"There is no greater agony than bearing an untold story inside you."
- Maya Angelou

Share Your Story

For centuries, stories have been the core of human interaction. Through them, we form invaluable bonds drawn by understanding, association, and empathy. By interpreting and sharing your own story, you'll be able to understand yourself better and realize your purpose as a person. But, as you live in a fast-paced world that is driven by complex things, do stories really matter?

The undeniable benefits that social beings get from sharing stories are countless. So, how can you start sharing your magnificent story?

1. **Start by believing in your story and its power to create a difference**

Owning and believing in one's story can be challenging for most. But it's the first step that you need to take to share your story with the world. If you think about it, it's more difficult to spend your whole life running from your own story than to embrace it and use it as a source of inspiration for others. Acknowledging your vulnerabilities may feel impossible, but if you don't, you'll miss out on the chance to find love, freedom, happiness, and belonging.

Start by sharing by believing in your story and its magnificent power to create a difference. Break the silence and begin a new inspiring chapter. All you have to do is listen and reflect on your own story, and acknowledge that every event has molded you to be the person you are. You are the only one who has the power to own and impart your story. If you're courageous enough to own it, then you'll be able to write a meaningful and purposeful ending as well.

How to believe your own story

♡ **Reconnect with your past, present, and future**

Whenever you reattach yourself to your truth, you'll realize that you are no longer a prisoner of your past. That your present doesn't worry you anymore, for it is another opportunity to get to know and better yourself, and that your future doesn't define and limit your potentialities. Rather, it is a window of hope and limitless possibilities.

By reconnecting with your past, present, and future, you'll be able to navigate the next chapters of your story with a heart full of hope and a mind of openness. By believing that you can choose to use the experiences that you encountered you'll be a better version of yourself and serve as an inspiration to others.

To Reconnect with your truth, you can start by reflecting on the following questions:

> What instances or experiences made you accept yourself as the worthy and amazing person that you are?
> What is the most inspiring thing that happened to you in life?
> Who/what inspires you and why?
> Was there ever a breakthrough moment when you recognized your inner strength?

♡ Accept and love yourself along the process

Accepting and loving yourself may be the most empowering thing that your story can bring. Your story, and the way you narrate it to others and yourself ultimately create your world. So, if you aspire to change the world you're in, then you need to change your perception of your story. But to do this, you need to love and forgive yourself first. Congratulate yourself for being able to come this far and for serving the purpose that it needed to fulfill.

To do this, you can start by reflecting on the following statements:

> My story matters because...
> I am worthy of...

♡ Be true to your core

The authenticity of your story is vital in conveying the message you want to impart. By remaining true to your core, you'll genuinely make others believe your story as well. Only when you start to own your identity and your experiences will you know what you're passionate about and what your purpose in life is.

To start connecting with your core, reflect on and answer the following questions:

> Why do you want to share your story?
> What insights do you want your listeners to learn from you?
> What do you want to stand for?
> Who were you a year ago? Today? A year from now?

"Owning our story and loving ourselves through that process is the bravest thing that we will ever do."
- Brené Brown

2. Focus on one thing or a single event that you consider special or remarkable

Focusing on one thing can make it easier for you to tell your story while holding your listeners' attention. It makes it more memorable for you and your audience as well. By focusing on a single memorable event, you'll also be able to convey your thoughts smoothly and without any hassle.

When you choose a topic close to your heart, you'll be able to carry out the insights that you'd like to express successfully. Genuinely, you'll be able to share what you want and receive the ideal feedback you're expecting to get.

3. Choose your audience

Knowing and choosing your audience will enable you to make sound decisions on the information and the narratives that you will include in your story, it will guide you as you arrange it, and will also give you a glimpse of the details that will be needed by your readers to understand it fully. Furthermore, it influences your narrative's tone, structure, and flow and allows you to develop and present your story effectively.

Knowing your audience also includes knowing their specific needs. By knowing how you can help them, you'll be able to write your story with a purpose and an end product in mind.

4. Know your purpose

"What is my purpose and goal for writing?" As a storyteller, this is one of the most essential questions you should ask yourself in sharing your story. Being in between the world of fact and fiction can sometimes shift your focus on your voyage, that's why you must have an established ground on what your purpose for sharing your story will be.

5. Write it down and imagine reading it to a friend

Whatever idea you have on your mind, whether it be your life story, or someone else's, may it be a story of hope and inspiration or happiness and adventure, the vital step you should take is to just write whatever you have in mind. Write it down on a piece of paper or encode it on your computer.

As you write your story, visualize yourself talking to a close friend. Say your words out loud and express your story as real and comfortable as you can. Write your story the way you naturally talk to your friend. By doing so, you'll be able to write a story from your heart and you'll be able to express your thoughts as authentically and genuinely as possible.

"After nourishment, shelter, and companionship, stories are the thing we need most in the world."
- Philip Pullman

Your story is incredibly important!

It doesn't have to be neatly wrapped in colorful bows; you just have to let people know that they are not alone, just like you. That you can all make a difference and form a connection strengthened by your stories of fear, desperation, anguish, struggles, and triumph, and guided by understanding, acceptance, and belonging.

As you share your story with the rest of the world, know that you hold the key to the life you desire. Do not allow yourself to be trapped in your story. Instead, let your story set you free. For your story doesn't end there.

Your tomorrow awaits you with hope and limitless possibilities. Your potential is greater than what you can imagine.

So, do you accept the challenge?

"Inside each of us is a natural-born storyteller,
waiting to be released"
- Robin Moore

Lynee Palacios

Chapter 11

Living A Life of Purpose

"You were put on this earth to achieve your greatest self, to live out your purpose, and to do it courageously."
- Steve Maraboli

We all have this innate yearning for a deeper sense of meaning no matter where we are walking in life. And as we journey in our own paths, we are faced with inescapable questions like, "Why am I here?" "What's my purpose in life?" "Am I living the life that was meant for me?" The truth is, without purpose, we'll feel that everything else is meaningless. For life isn't just about being alive. It's about living for something bigger, thriving for your truth, and making a difference in the world.

Finding one's purpose isn't just a far-fetched dream, nor an impossible ambition. It is an indispensable tool that will allow you to live a life of happiness, joy, freedom, and contentment. Searching for your meaning can be complex, especially now in this difficult time that we're in. And as each of us face our personal dilemmas and adversities individually, we are called to awaken and reflect on the long slumber that we've lived in and bring into being a new way of living.

I've always viewed life as a journey and an opportunity to do something remarkable, to create change, and inspire others. Even at a young age, I used to ask myself the bigger questions of my existence: "What impact do I want to make?" "What makes me feel most alive?" "What is my life's purpose?" and as I went through life and learned to follow my heart and my intuition, I found the consistent answer to all my "why's" in life. My calling lies in helping people find their purpose.

Through my life experiences, I understood that by helping one another, by giving love, compassion, kindness, and respect to those around us, and by inspiring others to do the same, we connect with our truth and our ultimate meaning.

Pause for a moment and reflect.

Reflect on today, yesterday, and the days to come.

Ask yourself this:

- Are you heading in the direction you're meant to go?
- Are you on your way to living your purpose in this world?

If your answer is Yes, congratulate yourself. Celebrate your small, unwavering, and courageous steps. Please, carry on. You're on your way. You're a work in progress and you'll soon see the worth of your efforts.

If you aren't in sync with your purpose and goals yet. Please, gently step off of your current track. You have the strength and potential to create a new and brighter path. Although it may seem like a long way, you'll eventually get there, and I promise you that it will all be worth it. You'll soon find your place and live the life you deserve and work hard for. Soon you'll get there.

"Everything can be taken away from a person but one thing: to choose one's attitude in any given set of circumstances, to choose one's own way"
-Viktor Frankl

How Can You Start Living Your Life Purposefully?

Living a life of purpose may seem highly implausible. But it shouldn't be, as we all can live our lives the way we like them to be. Let's look at the simple ways of achieving a more meaningful existence.

♡ Get in touch with your deepest whys

During your younger years, you make sense of and understand the mysteries of the world by asking your unending why's. From the smallest to the greatest questions you ask about the world, you develop the curiosity that will enable you to understand yourself, the situations you're in, and life in general. Your purpose in life also comes from the questions you ask and your existence becomes more meaningful with your unending queries. Having a strong sense of why in life guides you in living a life of purpose and meaning.

♡ Slow down and refocus

In life, it's essential to pause and reflect once in a while, for you to reevaluate the path you're on and ensure that you're living your life purposefully.

♡ Envision your life plans

Creating pictures in your mind about your life is essential in living a purposeful life. Having an end vision would serve as an everyday affirmation of the life you want to create. It will allow you to stay on track and avoid distractions throughout your path.

♡ Make conscious efforts

Living a life of purpose means making conscious choices in life and accepting whatever result it consequently creates. It is about being accountable for your own thoughts, actions, opinions, and decisions.

Knowing that you're in total control of your everyday life enables you to find peace and purpose in your existence. It also empowers you and makes you realize that you have the power to make your life the way you want it to be.

♡ Walk one step at a time

To live a life of purpose, you must realize that every morning you get to wake up is an opportunity to be better and to do better. Every step you take in your path towards success matters and contributes to your journey as a whole. So, ask yourself this every morning: "What small steps can I achieve today?" By doing this, you'll be able to walk more courageously and not feel overwhelmed by the things around you. You'll gain focus and perseverance along the way while staying gentle and accepting of yourself. You'll allow yourself to work at your own pace and avoid any distractions that may take you away from your goals. Your destination will remain clear and reachable through your everyday progress.

♡ Set your intentions straight

By setting simple goals for every waking day, you'll be able to choose the life you want and act for yourself to achieve it. Laying down intentions or objectives in life is clearly the most important step that one should take in living a purposeful life.

♡   Live in the moment

Living in the now is about being free from the baggage of the past and not having fears about what will happen in the future. It allows you to enjoy the present moment and live the life you deserve. Being present also permits you to see your purpose clearly and live in congruence with your goals without feeling too overwhelmed with your bigger dreams in life.

♡   Believe in yourself and trust life

Hurdles and challenges will inevitably be met along the way. Use them as your guide in your growth and progress as you live your life purposefully. For every hindrance that you might meet along the way, whatever form they may be, they are intended messages from life itself. All of them hold an important message, an invaluable lesson.

Take Action!

This challenge will help you as you start your voyage towards a more purposeful and meaningful way of living your life.

1. To get in touch with your deepest why's, situate yourself in your sanctuary. Sit comfortably, reflect and answer the following questions in your journal.

    What motivates you to get up every morning? What would you like to be remembered for?

Have you found your purpose in life?
Is your meaning or purpose in life in alignment with your present actions? What particular practices or habits get you closer to living your life's purpose each day?

2. Anytime during the day when you feel unmotivated, tired, or restless, strive to slow down and refocus, close your eyes and take a deep breath. Take a 3-minute break from any task that you're doing. Focus your attention on your breathing. Gently get in touch with your present thoughts, pay attention to why you're doing what you're doing, and with this awareness, continue your task with the vigor and motivation that you need to achieve your goals. Ask and remind yourself of your reason to keep going.

3. Create your vision board

    Goal setting is a process that can turn your plans and aspirations into real and attainable visions. By setting meaningful and unambiguous goals, you're able to cultivate your sense of direction, clarity of vision, and purpose in life.

    Making a vision board is one of the most helpful tools you can use to set goals and motivate yourself. Begin by creating a list of your major and minor goals, starting with the most important ones. This might include your personal, social, and professional goals, as well as your goals on health and fitness, followed by your hobbies and finances.

The next step is for you to search for images, words, or even other vision boards that you can identify with. You may find inspiration from magazines such as lifestyle, home, fitness, family, and others. It can also include colors, patterns, and textures that resonate with your personality or with the goals you've set your mind to. Once you have your images, theme, materials, and vision ready, all you need to do is put them together in an organized, pleasing, and effective pattern. You can start laying your images on a board of your choice. Arrange and layer them out first, and only when you're satisfied with how they are arranged, can you glue them on the board. You can also type and print or write notes around the pictures. By doing this, it will be more personalized and will have more sentimental value to you. You can use the note to reflect on where you stand and where you're heading in life.

After constructing your vision board, look for a place or an area that will always be accessible for your viewing. By placing it in a spot where you can see it anytime, you can create an opportunity that will train your mind and manifest your goals.

Have you discovered your life's purpose?

By being guided by a mission greater than yourself, you'll realize that every morning you wake up is an opportunity for you to make a difference in the world. A purposeful life isn't only defined by grandiose and heroic acts, it is seen in your everyday efforts to live a life intended for something worthwhile and to spark a change in someone else's life. So, live in the present moment and let your precious purpose and mission bring you focus and determination especially whenever the going gets tough and allow it to take you through life, leaving the past behind and facing tomorrow with your unwavering hope.

Go! The world awaits you!

"Learn to light a candle in the darkest moments of someone's life. Be the light that helps others see; it is what gives life its deepest significance."
- Roy T. Bennett

Lynee Palacios

To my dear readers,

Do you know how valuable you are?

There are more than 7 billion people in the world. Each carrying an extraordinary story, each going through a different struggle or celebrating a unique triumph. Knowing that you are living in the same world as the rest of its inhabitants may make you feel insignificant and small sometimes. But let me tell you an important message.

You're right on time

In your own unique path, in whatever time zone you follow, you are never late, you are not early. You are right on time. You may at times feel like you're left behind by your peers or by time itself. Let me tell you that you are not alone. Feeling lost and hopeless is an inevitable human experience, but please never forget that there's no deadline to finding your place in life. Just because you're taking a different route, doesn't mean you are lost. Celebrate the path of others, but most importantly, celebrate your path. You are right on time.

You are worthy

Of love, happiness, success, and all the wonderful things the world has to offer, you are worthy! Let me tell you that you and your feelings matter. From the tip of your toes to the top of your head, you matter, and if your reflection won't let you see that now, then, let me tell you that you are loved. You are valued. Even though you make mistakes. Even though you are far from being perfect. You are worthy of the love you freely give to others. Love yourself wholly, your flaws, your beauty, your strengths, and your imperfections. You are worthy.

You are enough

I know it has been a long day, probably a hard one too. So, I want you to stop for a minute and forgive yourself for all your shortcomings. You've been a little too hard on yourself. I know you've been beating yourself to grow and make your mark on this world, create a difference, but you need to be patient. For everything of value, would always take time to be built. You've just faced the dark clouds and now you're trying to find the right path. Know that you are enough; just as you are, just as you ought to be. You are enough.

Your existence makes a difference

They may say that you are just a speck of dust within the galaxy, a star among billions of others. It's true, I guess. But like the star that you are, your light contributes to the beauty that the sky holds. Your light illuminates the word in its darkness. Without you, the world would turn dim. Your existence makes a difference. Your presence alone can bring joy to someone. Your mere words can inspire a longing soul.

your passion can create something magnificent; your existence makes a difference.

You're an inspiration

Like a book, your life is full of chapters of triumphs and falls. There may be segments of your story that you'd like to erase, events too difficult or painful to talk about, that you would rather pretend didn't exist. Let this journey be a safe place where you can share your story and strive to be an inspiration to others. Allow the light to break the darkness that you're in so that you can clearly see that your existence and your story matter. You have the gifts that others might need. You are an inspiration.

You are never alone

Don't be afraid of what lies ahead. You've walked into so many unknowns in your life before that led you to where you are now. With what the world is going through, it's too easy for you to feel lost and alone. Please don't be scared. There are billions of people experiencing the same things, dealing with the same uncertainty, and facing the same unknown every single day. Around the world, though far apart, the world has never been so close. Please don't be scared, because you are and will never be alone.

With Love,

Lynee Palacios

"Live each day as if your life had just begun."
– Johann Wolfgang Von Goethe

About the Author

Lynee Palacios is a passionate and dedicated entrepreneur who started her journey in the fitness and nutrition industry. For over 13 years, she has competed in numerous fitness competitions and started several wellness businesses. In October 2008, she sold her organic meal prepping company to take on a full-time position working with Tony Robbins and Dean Graziosi as their Strategic Partnership Manager and Community Director. Their mission, along with over 22,000 community members, is to make self-education the new norm. She is extremely passionate about helping people reach their optimal health, achieve overall wellness, and live a life of purpose.

Lynee's pioneering spirit started as soon as she graduated from high school, where she worked and paid for her studies and earned a double major in Physiological Sciences and Human Nutrition. She then started a healthy meal prepping company in Scottsdale, AZ, and has helped countless businesses grow, such as Yeouth Skincare and Mastermind.com through social media affiliate marketing.

Her contagious energy provides a refreshing and motivating environment that her colleagues, along with the other 22,000 Mastermind community can attest to. Her passion for entrepreneurship and self-education is only matched by her love of traveling, learning about new cultures and cuisines, and appreciating life in its deepest form. She also loves interacting and connecting with people from different parts of the globe. As an established master networker, her true superpower is instantly connecting and

LYNEE PALACIOS

Entrepreneur
Motivational Speaker
Lifestyle & Business Coach
Health Coach & Registered Dietician
Strategic Partnership Manager
Community Director
A Grateful Daughter, A Well-loved
Sister & The Mother of Charlee

Scottsdale, Arizona

building rapport with anyone. Lynee has built online communities in New Zealand, Australia, Mexico, France, and Canada.

When Lynee is not behind her desk, you can find her on top of a mountain or scuba diving in the deepest ocean. Her heart, passion, and unparalleled dedication set her apart, and her caring and loving nature inspires those she comes in contact with.

At the moment she's a devoted mother to her little one, Charlee Sofia. She's Jamie Kern Lima's Community Director and the CEO of a Virtual Assistant Agency, myVIAA.com.

Made in the USA
Las Vegas, NV
28 December 2021